Searching for Intimacy

Searching for Intimacy

*Pornography, the Internet and the
XXX factor*

Foreword by Lyndon Bowring

Authentic

11 10 09 08 07 06 05 7 6 5 4 3 2 1

First published 2005 by Authentic Media
9 Holdom Avenue, Bletchley, Milton Keynes, MK1 1QR, UK
and PO Box 1047, Waynesboro, GA 30830-2047
www.authenticmedia.co.uk

British Library Cataloguing in Publication Data

A catalogue record for this book is available
from the British Library

ISBN 1-85078-585-6

Cover design by fourninezero design
Print Management by Adare Carwin

Contents

The authors

Dr Alice Swann, has worked for 25 years in the field of Child Abuse and Neglect. She has had a particular interest in the investigation and therapeutic intervention of Child Sexual Abuse, with a wide training remit here and abroad. For eight years she was an independent medical specialist appearing as expert witness in civil and criminal courts.

Dr Trevor Stammers is a GP in Wimbledon and an honorary senior tutor in general practice at St George's Hospital Medical School, London. He has written and broadcast widely on sexual health issues and has a regular series in *Trends in Urology, Gynaecology and Sexual Health*. He was the medical correspondent for the *Baptist Times* and a web-doctor for www.loveforlife. org.uk which responds to teenagers' enquiries about relationships and sexual health.

David Partington has worked in the addiction field since 1980 firstly as Director of Yeldall Manor Rehabilitation Centre and, until 1998, was CEO of Yeldall Christian Centres running a homeless project and prison based therapeutic programme. He is a founder member and General Secretary of ISAAC (International Substance Abuse and Addiction Coalition) which began in 1997. ISAAC is a network of 2,500 Christian individuals and projects in over fifty countries dedicated to impacting on the rapidly escalating problem of addiction around the world. David is the author of two books on addiction issues from a Christian perspective.

Stephen Carrick-Davies is Chief Executive of Childnet International, the children's Internet charity, established in 1995 to work with others to help make the Internet 'a great and safe place for children'. He has been responsible for developing the Childnet award-winning education and awareness resources such as 'Kidsmart' schools Internet safety education programme, and the international Childnet Academy programme. This seeks to reward children and young people who are developing outstanding Internet projects which benefit others. Under Stephen's leadership, Childnet is currently responding to the child safety issues of mobile technology and working with a number of organisations and companies round the world to ensure that the mistakes learned from the fixed Internet experience are not made by mobile operators. See www.childnet-int.org for full details.

Foreword

In October 2004 CARE hosted a day conference for church leaders entitled 'In Search of Intimacy' to look at ways in which the church could help Christians to escape the web of pornography. It was my privilege to chair the event. This book brings together the contributions of the distinguished conference speakers who helped us to understand the issue and offer hope to those affected by it.

From the beginning of creation, God designed sex as a good gift to bring fulfilment and pleasure in the security of a loving committed marriage relationship. '[He] saw all that he had made, and it was very good' (Gen. 1:31). Sadly in our fallen world, pornography sends the message to men and women that sexual faithfulness to one person is neither necessary nor satisfying.

For many years sexually explicit magazines, videos and books have been available on most high streets, but with the advent of the Internet a revolution in the delivery of pornography has come about. Today you can have access to any type of material imaginable whenever you want without even stepping outside your front door – and no one needs to know!

Unsurprisingly the numbers of men and women who are becoming addicted to pornography in general, and Internet porn in particular, are rapidly rising. It is seriously affecting Christians too – causing families to break up, young people to drop out of education, people to be dismissed from their jobs and many to feel guilty and depressed.

Prior to the 'In Search of Intimacy' conference CARE wrote to 3,000 church leaders about this issue and the results were deeply disturbing. Of the 1,200 replies received, 97 per cent indicated that they believed pornography to be a serious problem within the church. All had dealt pastorally with at least two people affected by it during the previous year. Eighty-six per cent said they lacked the resources to support them and a number confessed to having a problem with pornography themselves.

In response to this, CARE launched the website www.care.org.uk/anon to help Christians in this area. Thousands of phone calls and visits to this website have shown there is a vital need to offer practical support. One man expressed his appreciation, calling to say 'Thank God for CARE' having struggled alone for 20 years.

This book demonstrates that there is, in Christ, the possibility of release from the snare of pornography and that there is much that Christians can do to combat this destructive force in our society. It is our heart's desire to bring help and hope to those enslaved by it and draw them into a new walk of intimacy with God and a purity of heart. May He equip and encourage many of us to bring this about.

Lyndon Bowring
Chairman
CARE

The role of the Pornographic Industry in the destruction of intimacy

Alice Swann

In this modern world destruction on a massive scale is all too evident. A village is wiped out by a flash flood, genocide is ruthlessly planned and the Twin Towers collapse. All this, and more, diminishes us all. As Donne wrote: 'No man is an island, entire of itself: every man is a piece of the continent, a part of the main. If a clod be washed away by the sea, Europe is the less, ... any man's death diminishes me, because I am involved in mankind, and therefore never send to know for whom the bell tolls; it tolls for thee.'[1]

A less obvious form of destruction that diminishes us all is the destruction of intimacy in which the pornographic industry plays a large role. This industry exists to produce pornography, printed or visual material intended to stimulate sexual excitement. There are now opportunities, through the Internet, on a scale never known before to have access to this alluring world.

The negative aspects of pornography have been acknowledged by many including D.H. Lawrence who in an important publication stated 'Pornography is an attempt to insult sex, to do dirt on it.'[2] Christians have to respond but in doing so face many challenges.

Firstly, they must accept that pornography as an industry is successful and here to stay. For some people it is an acceptable way to communicate about sex. Those involved are making informed choices and indeed may not be or even regard themselves as being exploited. D.H. Lawrence (in the same essay) recognised that individuals vary in their perception of pornography: 'What is pornography to one man is the laughter of genius to another.'

It would be wrong, even harmful, for Christians seeking to help and understand others to immerse themselves in pornography but they may have to dip their toes into a very rough, seedy and shocking world.

Another challenge for us as Christians is to face up to what being created in God's image means in our view of ourselves, in our responsibility to others and our accountability to God.

Commercialisation: The pornographer is an exploiter and trickster

This is a market-driven industry intent on making as much money as possible. It is just not possible to accurately estimate the commercial value of pornography in general or Internet pornography in particular. What is clear is that this is a staggering industry in terms of profit, number of people involved and extent of distribution.

Whilst it is not possible to find accurate statistics Table 1 offers some indication.

This market place offers the user an ever-increasing range of readily available pornographic material and with it ever-increasing opportunities for the commercial distributors. One of the strategies available to the

TABLE 1

PORNOGRAPHY INDUSTRY STATISTICS

Adult videos	35%
Escort services	19%
Magazines	13%
Sex clubs	9%
Phone sex	8%
Cable/pay per view	8%
Internet	4%
Other	4%

Larger than Hollywood Industry. Larger than combined revenues of all football, baseball and basketball franchises. (USA)

INTERNET PORNOGRAPHY STATISTICS

Pornographic websites	12% of total websites
Daily porn search engines requests	25% of total requests
Worldwide visitors to porn websites	72 million annually
Average daily pornographic e-mails/user	4.5 per Internet user
Men admitting to accessing porn at work	20%
Women admitting to accessing porn at work	13%

Sources: Internet Filter Review www.internetfilterreview.com

distributor is to post material on the Internet to motivate customers to use pay-per-use bulletin board services. Chat rooms give users an opportunity to exchange information and ideas, including involvement in cyber-sex and interactive sex games.

Legitimate commercial outlets employ various techniques to attract and hold on to consumers. Some of these may even be aggressive and deceptive. Pornographers employ many such practices with the sole aim of deceiving or entrapping potential users.

One of the most common forms of deception is that known as 'cyber-squatting'. Pornographic sites use innocent sounding web domain names; for example, the best-known example of this is the confusion between the official site of the White House, Washington DC and a pornography site.

This industry is not about altruism, generosity, gentleness or liberty. It should be seen for what it is, a form of prostitution. Essentially it is about sex for money. As such it destroys intimacy.

Content: The pornographer is profane and obscene

The pornography industry, like any other industry, aims to meet its customers' needs and demands. What are these demands?

They are for sexual stimulation. More and more people are demanding more and more explicit images leading to not only an increase in availability but also an emphasis on a vast array of deviant sexual practices. This rapid growth is outstripping rules and regulations.

Pornography can be classified into two broad groups: soft core and hard core. Soft core pornography, whilst showing full nudity, does not emphasise violence or sexual perversion. Hard core pornography includes explicit display of genitalia and various kinds of sexual acts, many of which are exploitive, abusive, violent and denigrating.

Much is known about the content of pornographic magazines and films. However, there is little research into the content of Internet pornography. Mehta and Plaza carried out a study and a content analysis of pornographic images on the Internet.[3] The results suggested that commercial vendors are more likely to post explicit pornographic material in public access newsgroups to attract new customers to their private pay-per-use bulletin board services.

Results also suggested that the criteria for selecting what material was posted on the Internet was different from those used by magazine and video producers.

Most images appear to be taken directly from magazines and videos and there was a suggestion that the selection process represented the dominant interest of network users. It is then not surprising that the content is becoming more and more explicit.

Mehta and Plaza found that the most common themes were close-ups of genitalia, erect penises, fellatio and masturbation. Homosexual sex and group sex were more common in computer pornography than in other pornography.

Mainstream pornography is changing and with it a change in what is offered on the Internet. Sex feature films are becoming more pornographic. Some do not even attempt to have a story line, depicting extreme sexual activities often with violence. What is most concerning is a moral acceptance of what was once considered an unacceptable vice.

Pornography brings an unlimited hedonistic freedom for sexual expression, which fits easily in a society that wants more of everything, including sex. Pornography, which ignores boundaries, cannot really be considered an art form. This is in contrast to the discipline of true art form, whether it be a painting, book, film or poem. Wordsworth expresses this idea in a sonnet, 'Nuns Fret Not at Their Convent's Narrow Room'. He contrasts the satisfaction of those who have led a disciplined life to those who feel 'the weight of too much liberty'. Jesus, speaking of another disciplined life in his service paradoxically offers a yoke that is easy and light (Mt. 11:30).

For the Christian, sex is an intimacy within the boundaries of marriage characterised by, yes, passion but also by trust, respect and above all an over-riding desire for the good of the other. Pornography denigrates sexual acts, belittles the need for faithfulness and long-term relationships, throws off restraints and destroys any hope of intimacy that can be found in a committed sexual relationship.

Context: The pornographer exploits, profanes and tricks from the outside

Let us consider the meaning of pornography to those who use it by asking some questions:

Why do men and women use Internet pornography? The simple answer is for sexual stimulation, which may be even better than one could have with one's partner. There are an infinite number of possibilities presenting different sexual practices, some of which may be totally new to the user. There are many combinations that can fascinate someone used to a heterosexual relationship with one person. One can view male–female, male–male, female–female or group sex with seeming impunity.

How does a person use Internet pornography? It is usually in private. The person on most occasions will be masturbating whilst fantasising about the person on the screen, another desirable person or their partner. Very soon the images lose their ability to titillate or arouse so more explicit images are sought setting off an ever-increasing dependence on pornography.

There are more direct ways of becoming involved. The user can read and write explicit letters and stories. A visit to a sexually-orientated chat room may lead to an online affair. Now this person is contributing directly to Internet pornography.

What does this mean? Pornography allows an 'intimacy' outside the bounds of a faithful relationship. Elsewhere in this book the effect on the user and the spouse are considered. I would like to personalise those images used or, should it be said, misused, by all the players.

The true names, lives, hopes and aspirations of the men and women depicted, in whatever form, are often not known. Does that mean they are not real people? Does it mean that the user has no responsibility for them?

The challenge for the Christian is to think beyond the impersonal way in which the term 'image' is used. This pornographic image is a person who has a name, who is unique and who has been made in the image of God. We have all been made in God's image (Gen. 1:27) and as Boice[4] reminds us that means we have a responsibility to God, nature, others and ourselves. The 'others' include those men and women depicted on the screen who retain something of God's image and who are so valuable to God that they do not deserve to be so wantonly used.

Even though we are 'marred and shattered by sin' (Boice) we still have the ability to act in a responsible way. It is no excuse for the user to say, 'Someone else put it there. They are doing this willingly and getting well paid. I have a strong sex drive. I cannot help it. It's not as if I am having an affair.' Being made in God's image means we are moral agents in God's universe for others as well as ourselves.

The symbiotic relationship between users and pornographers is not evident because one acts in secret and the other openly. But it is there. They need each other, they take advantage of each other and one meets the needs of the other. It is a dance to someone else's tune and in this dance the destruction of intimacy has turned a full circle. The pornographers shamelessly play their parts in the destruction of intimacy. The users shamefully and irresponsibly play their parts in the wanton destruction of others also made in the image of God.

References

Boice, J.M., *Foundations of the Christian Faith* (Leicester: Inter Varsity Press, 1986)

Donne, J., *Poems and Prose* (London: Everyman's Library, 1995)

Lawrence, D.H., 'Pornography and Obscenity' in E. McDonald (ed.), *The Posthumous Papers* (New York: Viking, 1936)

Mehta, Michael D. and D.E. Plaza 'Content analysis of pornographic images available on the Internet' *The Information Society* 13(2), (1997): 153–162

The web of pornography

Trevor Stammers

For a libertarian, she seemed very keen to tell me what I should think and why I should think it! We were in the 'Green Room' after a tense live debate in Manchester in the wake of the murder of James Bulger. The spokeswoman for *Liberty* did not agree at all with my views on the power of television to influence behaviour. In the course of our subsequent, heated off-screen exchange on sex and violence, I mentioned that there is a difference between pornography and erotica. 'Huh!' snorted the spokeswoman. 'Erotica is merely what you like and pornography is what you don't.'

As a married man now approaching fifty, who still battles personally with the all-pervasiveness of pornography in most western societies, as a lecturer in addictive behaviour who has researched the effects of pornography for well over ten years and as a doctor (and sometimes friend) who has witnessed the tragedies of careers, marriages and families wrecked by pornography I have often thought about the spokeswoman's remark.

What makes something 'pornographic'? Is it just a matter of taste and personal opinion?

Pornography and erotica

Pornography is a slippery subject to define. The 1972 Longford Committee considered porn to be 'that which exploits and dehumanises sex so that human beings are treated as things and women in particular as sex objects'. [5]

This ties in with the Greek word *'porne'* meaning 'female captives' from which the word pornography (literally writing about *porne*) derives. Sexual material which degrades, or is violent, abusive or sadistic would be widely regarded as pornographic but what about sexually explicit material that is educational, artistic or simply non-violent? Are they any objective dividing lines between porn and erotica?

Nigel Williams, the current Children's Commissioner for Northern Ireland, suggests three questions which may be helpful in distinguishing the pornographic from the erotic

1. How does it portray women? (To which we must add, in the world of ever-increasing gay porn or porn for women, how does it portray men?) As people with personality or bodies to be lusted after?
2. How does it show sexual relationships? In relationships or in isolation?
3. What is the purpose of the material? Educational? Therapeutic?[6]

Judith and Jack Balswick in their comprehensive book *Authentic Human Sexuality*[7] consider that though both erotica and pornography are sexually stimulating, pornography always degrades and dehumanises whilst erotica celebrates human sexual experience.

They suggest that both the content and effect of sexual material should be used to determine if it is pornographic or not. With regard to content, degrading and de-humanising material is porn whereas affectionate and committed sex is erotica. Erotica gives meaning and value to sex whereas in porn, sex is just on the same level of moral value as eating a sandwich. On these criteria, the infamous sex scene between Julie Christie and Donald Sutherland at the beginning of the film *Don't Look Now* would probably be considered erotica, as the couple they portray are married.

In a recent and highly thought-provoking interview in *Third Way* magazine, Rowan Pelling, the editor of *The Erotic Review*, makes some interesting observations on the difference between erotica and porn

> To my mind, pornography is really clear what it's about: people pay a certain amount of money to get a certain amount of explicitness. It's all about what is within the frame. Imagination is not important. Erotica is very often about what you don't get, about how the mind goes beyond. There's always a human relationship between the photographer and subject, artist and subject … That's why I find the moral objection to erotica so strange, because without imagination every other kind of thing fails. You look at a bad housing project and you say 'Why didn't the architect show more imagination?' and yet people are very uncomfortable with the idea of imagination in sex.[8]

With regard to its effect on the viewer, however, what one person experiences as erotic, another may consider disgusting. The considerable amount of research suggesting that repeated exposure to even non-violent porn-ography desensitises and sexually disinhibits men (and to a lesser extent women) indicates that caution should be applied even with erotica.

Avoidance of all erotic material however would exclude us from many things that bring legitimate aesthetic pleasure and joy. Even within the Bible itself, the Song of Songs is surely an example of erotica which has profound spiritual merit? On a more mundane level, *Girl with a Pearl Earring* is one of the most erotic movies I have ever seen. There are no explicit sex scenes but the smouldering glances, the kneading of bread, a walk by the river, the mixing of paints – all these and more are charged with a powerful sexual undercurrent which permeates the whole film.

As well as taking into account matters of content and effect, I think one of the clearest distinctions between pornography and erotica and certainly between pornography and art, is that of the motivation behind it. My own definition of pornography is 'material made with the primary or sole intention that viewers should masturbate to it'. This may be a little simplistic but it can be very helpful in practice. The intention of the material's creator is usually clear and it is often obvious whether the film, book or website has any true artistic or literary merit. It is difficult to think of Botticelli's *Birth of Venus* for example as having the same primary purpose as a Page Three Girl picture.

Is pornography harmful?

Pornography is not usually immediately and directly harmful to most consumers but it lacks nearly all the elements of truly meaningful sex. These deficiencies can lead to serious problems in some cases. What are the important aspects of sex which are missing in viewing or masturbating with porn? In my book *The Family Guide to Sex and Intimacy* I list the following deficiencies.

Reality

Pornography is a fantasy world of stereotypes where the very beautiful women always have perfect and usually large breasts. The men are tall and oiled with sculpted pectorals and six-packs. Each image is designed to lead you to think that the next image will depict the ultimate body. It is the private world of make-believe that severs our links with the blemishes and flaws of the real world.

Yet while it can be stimulating on one level, there are subtle side-effects of such unreality which can be very unhelpful. How can you ever compete with such sexual perfection? Your body will never be like that. Those who feed on pornography starve their own sense of self-worth; the result is often depression.

The other obvious problem from frequent immersion in such a fantasy world is that any real sexual partner is unlikely to match the golden glow of Adonis or Venus either. How can anyone who has to pluck their eyebrows or, even worse, cut their toenails possibly compare with these god-like objects of worship that shine from the pornographic page?

Tim had been regularly watching porn on the net for years before he met and subsequently married Lucy.[9] Tim found making love to her almost impossibly distracting because she had several small but prominent moles on her back and thighs. Touching them was an instant turn-off for Tim because the girls he had sex with in his pornographic dreams all had perfect skin. The moles became mountains in his mind and he couldn't face coming to terms with the reality of Lucy's 'imperfections' so after a while he gave up and stopped any attempts at making love to her at all. Masturbating in front of the computer was much easier.

It was only several years after Tim sought help for his pornography addiction that he and Lucy were able to make love. Tim eventually found that not only did the moles no longer switch him off sexually, he stopped noticing them at all.

In the film *As Good as it Gets*, Helen Hunt plays a divorced waitress with a young son. There is a telling sequence where her boyfriend is attempting to sexually arouse her when her son calls out from his room. She goes in to see to him and the boy is sick all over her and his bed. She comforts him, cleans up the sick and returns to her frustrated and by now fuming would-be lover who tries again. On finding some vomit still on her blouse, he pulls his clothes back on and storms out of the door shouting that there was too much reality in the relationship.

In the real world, sex has both a context and consequences. Some of these are wonderful and good and some are horrific and harmful. One of the pornographic aspects of much sex education in our schools today is that quite aside from the explicit nature of some of the materials used, the overall message that is conveyed is that sex has either no consequences or they can be easily avoided.

To give the impression that the pill and the condom between them solve all problems is deception of the most cruel and dangerous kind. Condoms do not protect well against most of the common sexually transmitted infections (they do give good protection against HIV but this infection is comparatively uncommon[10] in the UK and USA). The pill can increase susceptibility to some infections such as Chlamydia. The studs and girls ever-ready for sex in the world of porn never get sexual diseases and in some popular sex education materials such infections are never mentioned either.

Relationship

In the search for intimacy, pornography is useless as a route map. Porn promises the ultimate but can never deliver the truly intimate. It doesn't usually even pretend to. Sexual partners strutting their stuff in porn movies never wear wedding rings. Relationship of any kind is usually so peripheral to the entire proceedings that often they don't even know one another's names before – or after – the performance.

> Pornography is concerned only with sensations, not with relationships and encourages their experience in isolation from the relationships to which they properly belong. It brings us into a world of irresponsibility where we can experience the emotional and some of the physical accompaniments of love-making without a partner and without any demand being made on all the other aspects of our personalities that we find being developed in a healthy marriage relationship.[11]

A few Christian couples have told me that viewing porn together does contribute positively to their actual relationship mainly in terms of acting as a sexual stimulus. However, porn inevitably focuses attention on someone else's partner at least initially and it can all too easily be counter-productive to intimacy by suggesting that the lover you don't have could be more exciting than the one you do. I have seen far more women whose husbands or partners have distanced themselves from their spouse by using porn than I have couples brought closer together by it.

Release

Sooner or later porn imprisons us. There is simply no comparison with the warm afterglow of intimate love-making (or the stabilising self-esteem of sexual abstinence) with the guilt-ridden dissatisfaction of the aftermath of masturbating to porn. Even in our sex-saturated culture where porn magazines are no longer 'top-shelf' material, porn is nonetheless often associated with guilt. Porn does not have pride of place on the coffee table in most homes – it's more likely to be hidden away in a drawer.

As one expert witness commented before the US Attorney General's Commission on Pornography

> The myth about porn is that it frees the libido and gives men an outlet for sexual expression which liberates mind and body. This is truly a myth. I have found that pornography not only does not liberate men but on the contrary is a source of bondage. Men masturbate to pornography only to become addicted to the fantasy. There is no liberation for men in pornography.[12]

Guilt cripples us so that we are unable to function normally or closely relate to other people. As one psychologist expresses it: 'As a therapist, I have found that guilt over sexual behaviour is a common cause of mental disturbance. Many who are active in the type of sexual lifestyle promoted by pornography seem to have lost something. The more sexually active they are, the less they enjoy it! One patient lamented "I seem to be dying inside".'[13]

The ideas that pornography encourages include

- A sense of excitement and escape from the routine of everyday life
- An illusion of sexual accomplishment and expertise
- Feelings of personal power and control
- Temporary relief from stress, anxiety, depression or feelings of loneliness and unattractiveness

- An intense but transient and fragmented thrill of personal pleasure.

However, as the feminist Susan Griffin bluntly puts it, 'If pornography were not a kind of mental addiction, an enthralled fantasy, who would seriously credit its "ideas"?'[14]

Respect
Quite apart from the guilt-inducing tendency just discussed, porn lowers self-respect in other ways.

It feeds the lie that the most important thing in life is having sex, and that you are missing out if you are not doing it as often as possible, and with as many partners as possible. It induces a constant nagging sense of deprivation which is an important predisposing factor for depression.

The fixation of porn on the sexual alone may hinder the development of other areas in character and personality which raise esteem and self-respect.

By his mid-teens, Sam was hooked on porn. From time to time he would make a really determined effort to break free from it and during one such bout threw all his magazines into a drainage ditch near his home. When the overwhelming urge to masturbate overcame him once again he climbed into the ditch to recover them. The literal mess he got into as a result mirrored to him the mess he felt inside and after this episode he sought counselling and eventually overcame his addiction. In the process he rekindled his neglected musical talent and joined a jazz band. Some years later through his involvement with the band he met his future wife. Pornography has not regained its grip five years on into married life.

Pornography can also stifle self-respect by its focus on self-centred sexual prowess rather than other-centred sexual fulfilment. Porn is concerned with technique not context. This can lead to considerable feelings of inadequacy. As psychologist Rollo May claims

> It is not surprising then, that in the preoccupation with techniques that the questions typically asked about an act of love-making are not, 'Was there passion or meaning or pleasure in the act?' but 'How well did I perform?' ... When people talk about the 'apocalyptic orgasm' I find myself wondering why do they have to try so hard? What abyss of self-doubt, what inner void of loneliness are they trying to cover up by this great concern with grandiose effects?[15]

Perhaps even more disturbing than the effect of pornography in eroding self-respect is its effect on respect for others. It has been said that the problem for women is in how the attitudes and behaviour of men who use pornography is affected; when women are portrayed in this way, how can they be taken seriously in society?[16]

In stereotyping women as 'always up for it', porn decreases men's sensitivity to their potential for an intimacy that involves relationship. This problem has been noted in several research studies. In one such study,[17] college students were exposed to standard non-violent pornography for one-hour sessions over six consecutive weeks. Following such exposure, these students had a greater tendency to trivialise rape, an increased acceptance of sexual infidelity and a decreased satisfaction in their partner's physical appearance and expressions of affection than students in the matched control group without such exposure to porn. These researchers concluded that the regular viewing of porn promotes increased callousness towards women in general and leads to decreased satisfaction with existing sexual relationships and diminished love toward an existing partner.

Nigel Williams graphically illustrates the human face of such academic research in his book *False Images*

> As we sat in the train in Manchester station three young football fans came into the compartment each carrying a pornographic magazine. As they sat down in the seat behind us we could hear them talking about the contents ... Then a very attractive young woman joined the train and sat level with my companion and me. One of the fans looked up from the magazine and said to the others in a sniggering tone, 'Cor. Look, a woman.' It is hard to convey in the printed word the degree of sexual undertone he managed to invest in that short phrase. I know if I had been that young woman I would have felt very intimidated by those young men.

The lack of respect of those who run the porn industry even for their own workers was dramatically highlighted in April 2004 when Darren James, a veteran porn actor, tested positive for HIV in screening routinely carried out every few weeks by the Adult Industry Medical Healthcare Foundation. Filming was stopped immediately for 60 days during which another three of the 45 others who had been in scenes with him tested HIV positive. Los Angeles health authorities called for the mandatory use of condoms throughout the industry which makes 4,000 films a year and employs 6,000 people. Did the producers co-operate in order to protect their employees?

The majority reacted by calling the idea an attack on their business and the quality of their films. Many studios centred on San Fernando, north of LA, said they would simply move out of California rather than comply as 'there are a lot of people who don't like to watch movies with condoms'.

As a result, AIDS activists picketed the offices of Larry Flynt, one of the best known porn kings in Beverly Hills, carrying placards proclaiming 'Latex now Larry!' Flynt declined to answer the protesters in person. However in a written statement he asserted that the industry should not have a condom rule, echoing his belief that 'safe-sex' productions were harmful to profits. Performers, who are mostly hired by the scene, said that when they insisted on using condoms, they were rarely hired again.

This is the kind of concerned and loving attitude for its own that characterises porn-makers. Those who use their products should realise what kind of people they helping to make rich.

Restraint

The addictive potential of porn is high and many who get hooked on it find themselves being drawn far deeper into a well of obsession and misery than they could have imagined when they first started. High court judges, prominent businessmen, concert pianists and evangelical pastors have all been among those caught in the recent sting operation on users of child porn sites. What perhaps quite honestly begins as a search for personal intimacy can end in an agony of mental and possibly literal imprisonment.

There are still psychiatrists and counsellors who confidently claim that there is no convincing evidence that pornography has any undesirable consequences but such claims are increasingly difficult to maintain.

The US Attorney General's Commission on Pornography was unanimous in its finding of a causal link between porn and sexual violence. John Court, former Professor of Psychology at Flinders University in Australia, wrote a paper of which the title said it all: 'Pornography and Rape: Promise and Fulfillment'.[18]

Another psychologist, Floyd Winecoff, testifying at the Minneapolis hearings on pornography, stated as far back as 1983 that 'Pornography portrays a fantasy of social communion, but in reality it leads to the desperation that leads to abusiveness'.[19] In the UK, Ray Wyre, former Director of the famous Gracewell Clinic and a world authority on sexual offenders, asserted 'In the course of my work I have developed a model which identifies the patterns which predictably operate in the cycle of sexual abuse. I have discovered that pornography can and does function at every stage in that cycle.'[20]

The truth of Wyre's conclusion is well illustrated by the extreme but not unique case of Ted Bundy. A convicted serial killer and rapist, the night before his execution in 1989 he was interviewed by Dr James Dobson. Bundy stated 'I'm no social scientist and I haven't done a survey but I have lived a long time in prison now. And I've met a lot of men who were motivated to commit violence just like me. And without exception every one of them was deeply involved in pornography.' [21]

True, the risk of such a steep escalation is very small for most people, and Bundy's acts are a far cry from renting a porn DVD from your local shop. However, the link is there and heavy consumption of common forms of porn fosters an appetite for stronger materials. For Christians called to live a life that is an example to unbelievers, can we afford to take the first step down that road? And in the development of true intimacy with our spouse or partner, will watching porn help or hinder this process?

The lack of restraint that characterises porn is now increasingly seen in alleged sex education in schools. As sexual health measures in the UK continue to worsen, those who have fuelled the process by promoting 'value-free' sex education at secondary school level now maintain the only answer is to push their propaganda onto primary school children as well. A mum recently told me how concerned she was when her nine-year-old daughter came back from school and excitedly told her what she had learned in a sex education lesson at school that day: 'I learned why the man has to go up and down and I learned why condoms are flavoured so they taste nice on the man's penis.' I expressed my own concern to the House of Commons Health Select Committee recently that the line between sex education and child abuse can in some schools be dangerously thin – a conviction affirmed by the fact that sex education leaders campaigned vigorously to be exempt from prosecution over the offence of assisting under-age sex when the recently proposed Sexual Offences Bill was debated. The glazed look of incredulity and incomprehension that came over the MPs' faces shocked me to the core. They simply could not understand what I was talking about.

Take for example the following quotes from two popular sex education resources from the USA which are quite modest in comparison to some of the government recommended materials over here. [22]

> Invite students to brainstorm ways to increase spontaneity and the likelihood they'll use condoms … e.g. Use condoms as a method of foreplay … think up a sexual fantasy using condoms … act sexy when putting the condom on … tease each other manually while putting on the condom.
>
> State that there are other ways to be close to a person without having sexual intercourse. Ask youth to brainstorm ways to be close. The list may include … body massage, bathing together, masturbation, sensuous feeding, fantasising, watching erotic movies, reading erotic books and magazines …

In other contexts such suggestions would constitute grooming if initiated by a paedophile but in the class-room this is all quite acceptable in the name of reducing sexual risk-taking. Pornography is a big enough problem outside school without initiation into its use in the classroom.

Sexual addiction

To look at Simon, or even to work with him or know him as a neighbour or acquaintance, you would not know he was an addict. Neither would I and I have been his GP for more than ten years.

He's tall, well-built and sports a perma-tan. He has a well-paid responsible job in the City. He's good at it and he knows it. He always seems very happy and laughs and jokes through the few consultations I've had with him over the years.

His wife is beautiful with a sparkling personality and they have a young daughter who is as bright and effervescent as any toddler could be. Yet his addiction is ruining his life and his family and he is content to let it do so. His wife can stand it no longer and has said that it's a choice between it and her. He doesn't see it that way, though. His habit has done him no harm that he can see and he thinks she is making unreasonable demands in begging him to quit it.

Family breakdown, and tension and conflict in close relationships are just two of the many harmful social consequences of addiction. In Simon's case the addiction is to cocaine but from his story it could just as easily be to Internet porn – often referred to as the 'crack cocaine' of porn addiction.

Symptoms and signs of pornography addiction

Though there is still some opposition to the whole concept of behavioural (as opposed to substance) addictions, there is now a huge proliferation of academic and popular writing which considers a wide variety of behaviours as potentially addictive. These include gambling, eating, exercising and shopping as well as various sexual addictions including use of pornography.

The behavioural addictions including porn addiction demonstrate the core components of substance addiction – salience, mood change, tolerance, withdrawal, conflict and relapse.

Salience refers to the tendency of porn to dominate the person's life. The addict becomes increasingly preoccupied with preparations for and viewing pornography and masturbating to it. Increasing amounts of time are taken up with these activities and strong feelings of desire to do them (*cravings*) may be present at other times. While not actually viewing porn, the addict's thoughts may be fixed on the next time they will be. One study of over nine thousand Internet users[23] found that 8 per cent spent more than eleven hours per week on sexual pursuits online. Work or family obligations can be neglected as a result and there may be a deterioration of social behaviour such as anger welling up when the user is interrupted.

Mood modification is the subjective change that users report in response to porn. Such feelings include a 'high' – usually just before or at the point of orgasm or conversely a sense of 'numbness' or 'escape' from realities too tough to face up to in day-to-day life. This is why most men are more vulnerable to engage with porn when under stress at work or at home.

Tolerance is the name given to the mechanism whereby the usual doses of a drug no longer give the same effect on repeated use and the dose has to be increased in order to get the same effect. The same process usually occurs in porn addiction where increasingly hard core material is need to stimulate a sexual response or alternatively increasing amounts of time are spent looking for novel material.

Withdrawal symptoms may be experienced when certain drugs are stopped suddenly. Similar patterns of feelings or symptoms such as irritability or shaking may develop when porn is not available.

Conflict can result in three areas – in relationships with others, especially with a spouse or sexual partner, at work when porn use depresses productivity and efficiency, or internal conflict when the addict's conscience breaks through and they feel uncomfortable with what they are doing. Internal conflict may be particularly destructive among Christian porn addicts.

Relapse is the tendency to revert to harmful patterns of porn use, for example during times of stress, even after many years of abstinence.

Internet addiction

Given the damage that can be done by pornography in general, why is the Internet considered as the 'crack cocaine' of pornography and does it pose particular risks?

One of the major factors which enhance the danger of Internet pornography is its anonymity. This means that

- the embarrassment of going into shops to buy pornography or the risk of being seen doing so by a fellow-church member is eliminated

- the viewing of deviant, bizarre and even criminal sexual acts is facilitated.

Another obviously important factor is its accessibility.

- Most shops or other porn outlets close at some point but the Internet provides access to it 24 hours a day, seven days a week. It is instantaneous with no waiting as with mail order
- The amount of material available is infinitely varied. This leads to increased use and a tendency to access material that otherwise might not be purchased. The line between erotica and frankly criminal material such as child pornography can be very thin and search engines do not distinguish between sites well.

Affordability is another aspect of Internet pornography. There are thousands of pornographic sites which are free and with most net users having a fixed monthly payment for unlimited use accessing porn for nothing is easy.

Easy access and affordability combine to make up some sobering statistics on use of the Internet for sex.

- The word 'sex' is the most popular search term used
- The US porn industry nets 15 billion dollars annually
- It releases 10,000 new titles a year (compared to 400 mainstream Hollywood movies)
- A third of UK Internet users access porn online
- A quarter of all UK internet traffic goes to porn sites and 70 per cent of this occurs at work
- One in four ten to seventeen-year-olds reported encountering unwanted Internet porn in the previous year
- One in five had been exposed to unwanted online sexual advances

- Four out of ten pastors in a USA survey admitted visiting porn sites.

The Internet also offers the other options for sexual stimulation that are not possible with previously available media. Manipulations of images or interactive involvement in cyber-sex games are unique to computer porn and the development of sexual relationships online is another potent source of addiction.

Disinhibition is another feature of the net – as anyone who has bolted off a hasty e-mail has cause to know. With regard to online chat rooms, users often open up more quickly and reveal their secrets and desires more readily than in face-to-face personal encounters. Thus, online intimacy of a sort may develop in hours or weeks to a level that would normally take months in an offline romance.

Chat rooms can also foster a totally unreal atmosphere of trust when body language and non-verbal clues which might otherwise give some warning signals are not part of the interchange. Deliberate deception is of course another danger and the online persona may not match the reality of the individual concerned. And even those who start off with a more innocent agenda can find the worlds of cyber-relationships one which easily encourages experimentation with fantasies. For those curious about a whole range of sexual behaviours such as what it is like to have sex with someone of the same sex, the Internet provides a place to explore these ideas anonymously. The possibility of linking up with those that one would not be likely to meet in the course of everyday life also enhances the attraction of the Internet for those whose sexual lives seem unfulfilling.

Such 'online affairs' constitute a whole new dimension of possible infidelity within marriage. Traditionally, marital unfaithfulness has involved a physical sexual relationship outside the marriage. Internet sex, however, has shifted the boundaries and wives or husbands uncovering an online sexual liaison may regard it in the same way as a conventional affair. It can be highly damaging to the future of their marriage. Furthermore, in one of the few research studies on the partners of cyber-sex addicts one-fifth reported that their partner's online affair progressed to an offline physical relationship.

Though there is considerable overlap in the way that men and women use cyber-sex there are important differences. Men are much more likely to be consumers of cyber-sex and it has the perceived advantage of removing performance anxiety associated with such problems as premature ejaculation. Men are also much more likely to access newsgroups which facilitate exchange of porn pictures.

Women, however, rarely if ever use newsgroups but prefer chat rooms suggesting that even online women seek sexual outlet in the context of 'relationship'. Even so, women who prefer cyber-sex often do so because it removes the social stigma that can attach to women who enjoy frequent sex and it forms a safe haven for them to concentrate on their sexual activity in an uninhibited way.

The currently few academic studies into cyber-sex addiction have shown that only a small minority of those engaging in sexual activity on the Internet will suffer major consequences. Of those that do, nearly all are men and around a third to a half are married. Men with a bisexual or homosexual orientation are also more at risk and over three-quarters of men had a substance addiction as well. Two-thirds of women with Internet sexual addictions had a history of sexual abuse and/or had an eating disorder in addition.

Children and Internet pornography

There is very little published research on the sexual use of the Internet by children and adolescents. Given the high sexual drive of those entering puberty and the fact that Internet use is also high in this age group it would be surprising if the problems affecting adults bypassed teenagers altogether. It is likely that pornography addiction and other cyber-sexual activity is increasingly common in teenagers and even younger children.

Untangled from the net – Treatment

The goal of treatment for some addictions, particularly alcoholism, is lifelong abstinence. However for Internet addiction, total abstinence from computer use is not a realistic long-term goal in a society that will inevitably see increasing incorporation of computer use into our everyday lives. Rather the goal is to restore a healthy normal sense of self-worth, and sexual understanding and expression much in the same way that a normal eating pattern can be restored to bulimics and anorexics.

The first step in seeking treatment, however, is recognising that you have a problem. Is pornography really something God opposes?

God on porn

In 1991 Nigel Williams, in his book, *False Images – Telling the truth about pornography*, wrote: 'we should not be surprised that some Christian men (and some women too) have a problem with pornography'. More than a decade later, I am frankly surprised these days if I meet a

Christian man who does not have (or has had) a problem with pornography. The only thing that surprises me is that quite a few do not acknowledge it as a problem and do not see its dangers.

The Bible of course does not mention pornography as such, but it does have a lot to say about *'porneia'* (translated generally as 'fornication', 'whoredom' or 'sexual immorality'), the Greek root similar to that from which pornography gets its name. The Bible also has much to say about purity and integrity – qualities that pornography sooner or later destroys.

There are 26 New Testament references to *porneia*, six of them occurring in Paul's letter to the church at Corinth. In the sexually addicted culture of that city, Christians were under as much pressure to conform to social norms as we in the west are today. Yet Paul tells these Christians (and us) that our bodies are not made for *porneia* (1 Cor. 6:13), that we should run from it when it comes looking for us (v. 18), that we should avoid going looking for it (1 Cor. 7:2), and that if we do succumb to its lure, it is something we need to repent of (2 Cor. 12:21) rather than being complacent about. It should be something abhorrent to followers of Jesus, yet Paul suggests that problems with *porneia* in the Corinthian church had reached an extent that even pagans would not generally talk about! (1 Cor. 5:1)

Purity is the very opposite of *porneia*, and though purity is not by any means restricted to the sexual in its scope, it is in this arena that most Christians (in the west at least) find the greatest difficulties in remaining pure. Paul urges Timothy, his young protégé, to keep himself pure (1 Tim. 5:22) and encourages the Philippian Christians to focus their thoughts on things that are pure (Phil. 4:8) (and it takes some fancy theological footwork to fit porn into that category). Most Christians are also aware that Jesus' blessing is on the pure in heart (Mt. 5:8).

In Ezekiel chapter 8, there is the chilling story of God's layer by layer exposure of the full extent of the hidden decadence of Israel's spiritual leaders. The 'idol that made the LORD so angry' (v. 5) was probably that of Asherah, the Canaanite goddess of fertility whose worship entailed *porneia* and self-gratification. God instructs Ezekiel to peek initially through a hole in the wall to see what the leaders 'are doing with their idols in dark rooms ... saying "The LORD doesn't see us"' (v. 12, New Living Translation). However, nothing is hidden from God's eyes and eventually the whole wall is torn away exposing the evil within. God still sees and grieves over the deeds done in dark rooms illuminated by the seductive glow of pornographic images today. Christians sensitive to God's Spirit, who are caught up with Internet and other forms of pornography, need to seek help to get free from it.

Face up to the fact that you are addicted. The locked drawers, the programs to prevent accessed sites being traced, the secret credit-card account – they all point to it. If you still need convincing there are quite a number of questionnaires available to assess whether you have a problem or not. Why not spend a few minutes completing this one taken from the CARE website:

1. Do you regularly spend time looking for sexual stimulation on the Internet (pornography, sexual/ romantic chat rooms, etc.)?
2. Have you tried to stop your involvement with Internet pornography, but have been unable?
3. Does your involvement with Internet sex interfere with your physical well-being (e.g. being tired from staying up late viewing Internet pornography)?

4. Have you masturbated while watching Internet pornography or immediately afterwards?

5. Do you hide your involvement with cyber-sex from your spouse or others close to you?

6. Are you preoccupied during the day with sexual fantasising, based on images or experiences you have had on the Internet?

7. Do you try to avoid social engagements, or try to leave such engagements early in order to spend more time involved in Internet sex?

8. Have you logged on to Internet sex sites from your computer at work?

9. Have you felt shame or depression following involvement with cyber-sex?

10. Do you feel guilty in the sight of God because of your involvement with Internet pornography?

11. Are you less involved with your spouse or close friends because of your involvement with cyber-sex?

12. Have you lied to/sought to cover up from your spouse or others about your use of Internet pornography?

13. Has your family or friends complained about the amount of time you spend online?

14. Do you frequently become angry and irritable when asked by family or friends to decrease your involvement with the Internet?

Interpretation:
'Yes' on 1–3 questions indicates you may have a problem. More than three positive answers indicate that you may have a more serious problem. Refer to the list of things you can do below for some help.[24]

Repentance and accepting forgiveness
Having acknowledged the problem, where do you go from there? In virtually every field of addiction from

drugs to gambling, from sex to smoking you will find that the Twelve Steps, principles developed originally by Bill Wilson, the founder of Alcoholics Anonymous, will be suggested. They are such a widespread concept in recovery from addiction that they are printed in full below.

1. We admitted we were powerless over *self-destructive behaviour* – that our lives had become unmanageable.
2. Came to believe that a Power greater than ourselves could restore us to sanity.
3. Made a decision to turn our will and our lives over to the care of God *as we understood him.*
4. Made a searching and fearless moral inventory of ourselves.
5. Admitted to God, to ourselves, and to another human being the exact nature of our wrongs.
6. Were entirely ready to have God remove all these defects of character.
7. Humbly asked him to remove our shortcomings.
8. Made a list of all persons we had harmed, and became willing to make amends to them all.
9. Made direct amends to such people wherever possible, except when to do so would injure them or others.
10. Continued to take personal inventory and when we were wrong promptly admitted it.
11. Sought through prayer and meditation to improve our conscious contact with God *as we understood him,* praying only for knowledge of his will for us and the power to carry that out.
12. Having had a spiritual awakening as the result of these steps, we tried to carry this message to others, and to practise these principles in all our affairs.

Though couched in general terms the first seven steps are from a Christian perspective, all about repentance and confession – recognising that we are in trouble, unable to get ourselves out of it in our own strength but determined to change with God's help. This is an essential component. I remember the evening some twenty years ago now when after years of battling with pornography, God gave me such a conviction of his pain over my sin, but also of his willingness to forgive it and to set me free from it. It was a turning point and I was on the road out of the darkness.

Confession to God (Ps. 32:5) may in this arena also be helped by confession to another trusted Christian friend or counsellor (Step 5). The principle of 'confess your sins to one another' (Jas. 5:16), though given in a different context and easily abused, can nevertheless be of enormous help in the area of healing from sexual sin. Admitting the full extent of pornography addiction is very difficult; the temptation to minimise the problem or hide important aspects of it is always there. However fully exposing the issues to the light in this way means that healing can be as deep as it needs to go and the chances of relapse are reduced.

Freedom is a process

The crisis of confession and repentance is of course just the beginning and remaining free is a lifelong process. Steps 8–12 recognise this and form part of a long-term strategy to achieve it.

Details of many helpful specific strategies to escape the net of porn can be found on the CARE website and in many of the references for this chapter. My own experience is that two components are essential however.

a) Accountability

Pornography is like quicksand and few can pull themselves out without help. Sharing our weakness with someone else who will support and pray for us is invaluable. Finding the right person though can be difficult. Spouses are rarely appropriate as they are too easily wounded by our actions to be in a position to offer the degree of neutrality required.

The person we share with needs to be understanding and able to encourage us but they also need to be objective and at times challenging so they do not collude with our sin! I have several people to whom I am accountable in this area and the most helpful is a wonderful woman in her seventies who is ruthless with me and of whom I have an affectionate and healthy fear. Telling her if I had culpably sought out porn was a most excruciating business and a very effective deterrent for me. Sometimes men can be a bit too sympathetic with one another!

b) Avoidance

We need to steer clear of situations in which we are likely to view pornography. One vicar I know found that if staying in a hotel room alone, taking the aerial out of the TV in his room and locking it in the boot of his car was an effective way of avoiding problems. Having a filtering package installed on the PCs at home and work may also be a useful move.

Sometimes a period of avoiding even activities which ordinarily would be quite legitimate but which weaken us is needed. One of my passions is musical theatre and cinema but I once cut all trips to shows and cinema for a few months until the drive to watch porn was under control. Even though the film may be pure, often the trailers and ads which accompany it will not be.

Avoidance of unhelpful fantasy and thought patterns is also important. Paul (again in addressing the Corinthian church) tells us that to 'take captive every thought to make it obedient to Christ' (2 Cor. 10:5). This has to be done at an early stage with pornography. It is easier to take captive the thought 'I will just click and see what I might find' than to take captive the thought 'Just one more picture won't make any difference'.

Catastrophising or exaggerating the problem in your mind is a well recognised thought pattern in addicts. 'I can never live without porn' is a typical example. This needs to be faced and acknowledged as the lie that it is and replaced with a positive thought such as 'My self-respect and sense of well-being will increase once I am free from this', or 'My wife and I have a chance to value each other more once all this stuff is out of my head'.

Though initially changing our thinking can be an emotionally draining and exacting discipline, it does become an almost reflex way of life after a while. Even in this area of life his 'yoke is easy and [his] burden is light' (Mt. 11:30) – at least in comparison with the burden that porn makes us carry.

Pornography is a sexual cul-de-sac. It goes nowhere worth the price paid in getting there. As John Court expresses it

> To reject pornography is to take a stand for sex as a special way of expressing and deepening interpersonal commitment. Pornography fails to understand sex as a sacred gift intended for joy, intimacy and deep fulfilment in a loving lasting relationship.[25]

Those who discover the joy and life from that sacred gift will find the plastic substitute of porn losing its power over them.

References

Balswick, Judith K. and Jack O., *Authentic Human Sexuality* (IVP, 1999)

Court, Prof. John, *Pornography – A Christian Critique* (IVP, 1990), p. 82

Griffin, Susan, *Pornography and Silence* (Women's Press, 1981), p. 20

Griffiths, Richard, *Art, Pornography and Human Value* (Grove, 1976), p. 21

Lord Longford, *Pornography: The Longford Report* (London: Coronet Books, 1972), p. 412

May, Rollo, *Love and Will* (Dell, 1969), p. 944

Stammers, Trevor, *The Family Guide to Sex and Intimacy* (Hodder & Stoughton, 1994)

Williams, Nigel, *False Images – Telling the truth about pornography* (Kingsway, 1991)

Recommended reading

Arterburn, Stephen and Fred Stoeker, *Every Man's Battle* (Waterbrook Press, 2000)

Arterburn, Stephen, Fred Stoeker and Mike Yorkey, *Every Young Man's Battle* (Waterbrook Press, 2002)

Recommended websites

www.care.org.uk/anon
www.iprodigals.org

The whole world in children's hands

Pornography, children and the Internet

Stephen Carrick-Davies

The Internet puts the whole world in children's hands.
Photo: Stephen Carrick-Davies

Preface

Any analysis of the impact of pornography on our society, and the way in which the Internet has increased our exposure to it, needs to include a review of the way in which children are vulnerable and the challenge that parents face in helping children and young people stay safe whilst using the new powerful interactive communication tools. In his chapter, Stephen Carrick-Davies, the Chief Executive of Childnet International* – the children's Internet charity – examines the way in which children are increasingly exposed to pornography online and the ways in which this material can be used to sexualise them. The chapter concludes with a challenge to the church to both support parents and young people, as well as work with and challenge other sectors to ensure that children's rights are protected and promoted.

*Childnet is not a Christian organisation though was established on Christian values.

'No one knows you are deaf on the Internet!'

A friend of mine called Tomi[26] loves the Internet. At sixteen years old he is truly a member of the digital revolution and has spent most of his teenage years seamlessly integrating the amazing communication tools into his everyday life. With the whole world in his hands he's been able to connect to friends, information, entertainment and creative resources all from the comfort of his family sitting-room computer.

Tomi was one of the first people I knew to get a camera phone and the first to take a digital picture of me using this phone. At the time I marvelled as he showed me the colour screen and the range of new features. For Tomi, this was far more than just a phone: it was his alarm clock, his address book, e-mail browser, camera, FM radio, as well as his tool to text his parents so they could pick him up, and his link with latest results of a TV reality show.

However, for Tomi, the Internet access and his mobile phone are even more important than for other children, for Tomi is deaf. As he told me when I took his picture, 'No one knows you are deaf on the Internet!' So whilst as a young person using these powerful technological tools Tomi is vulnerable and able to access potentially un-welcome content and come into contact with strangers, the Internet for Tomi is also a 'bridge' to the outside world and has opened up to him enormous opportunities for positive, creative communication which have quite literally changed his life for good.

Tomi's use of the Internet – and now mobile phones – mirrors that of other young people not just in the UK but increasingly throughout the world. In Nigeria – where Tomi was born – children and young people in the cities are eager to 'leap-frog' a generation of technology and are craving the new mobile handsets which will give them access to the whole world through their fingertips – a world their parents would never have dreamed of accessing or interacting with.

'Putting the genie back in the bottle!'

It may seem strange to start an article about the dangers of children using the Internet (and pornography in particular) with Tomi's story, but I do so because it illustrates so clearly the dilemma and challenge of the new technologies. On the one hand there is so much potential opportunity and benefit for children, especially those who are isolated, in using an amazing communication tool. A tool which has the power to unlock learning and allow children to share their own learning resources. However, on the other hand children are vulnerable and can access inappropriate content, including a virtual quagmire of pornography, in what is largely an unregulated medium.

Whilst the term 'digital divide' is often overused[27] in the context of access and equality, the new technologies are creating another digital divide – the one between parents and their tech-literate kids who are now using the technology applications in quite different ways.[28] For example, most adults use the Internet at work or home for researching, finding information and communicating via e-mail. Children, on the other hand, largely want the interactive features of instant messenger, chat rooms, competitions, and games, and in this way access a whole range of content that is increasingly interactive without the safeguard of parental supervision.

What's challenging about looking at this subject is that the speed of change is phenomenal and the dangers are multiple and increasingly overlapping. This is challenging to parents who recognise that their children have greater knowledge and understanding of the new tools. However, being 'tech-literate' is very different from being 'life-literate'. Parents cannot put the technology genie 'back into the bottle'. Instead they need to seize the opportunity to learn from their children, share their new world and help educate their children to use these powerful tools safely, as well as understand the nature of the material they will encounter. This will include understanding the nature of pornography, and its impact. This involves us as parents making tough choices, doing our homework and being disciplined, or is that something which we only want to foster in our children?

Page Three to 3D pop-up

The Internet has helped catapult pornography into our everyday mainstream culture. It has put 'Page Three' into 3D and sadly for some has become synonymous with the 'START' menu on the browser. Despite the very real concern of child pornography on the Internet (or to use its more accurate term – child abuse images) there has been scant regard for the interests of children in the debate of legal pornography online, save for an under-funded Internet content rating system and a plethora of commercial filtering technologies which have varying degrees of effectiveness and require constant updating.

It is as if we have forgotten the call from one of the founders of the Internet, Tim Berners-Lee, who wrote 'The web is more a social creation than a technical one. I designed it for social effect – to help people work together – and not as a technical toy ... We have to ensure that the society we build with the web is the sort we intend.'[29] Whilst we accept that censorship of this global medium is impossible, we have to admit honestly that the rampant growth of pornography on the Internet and its accessibility for children has not helped create a society which most parents would intend for their children.

Whilst the Internet is unique in privatising the consumption of pornography and offering us greater anonymity, it merely reflects a greater acceptance and accessibility in our society. Indeed other media and high street outlets have helped remove the harshness of pornography and disguised it as simply a life-style choice; something you can order along with your take away meal or purchase as easily as a new 'FCUK wet dream' T- shirt.[30]

Tom Cruise, who has steered a careful career and been in the media gaze for most of his adult life, captured this challenge when he said recently in an interview that some people didn't know what their own moral code was until they betrayed it.[31] As a barometer of our own moral code, our own private use of the Internet can serve as a powerful mirror and gauge for our own personal behaviour.

As a father myself I wonder how I can protect my young children from excessive marketing and com-mercialism, some of which unapologetically seeks to sexualise young people at an early age. I'm challenged that as I try to protect them from seeing pornography I am being re-sensitised and called to examine my own moral code. As I think more deeply about it, as I have for this article, I am somewhat shocked at the way in which I have become immune to so many of the semi-porn images along with my generally watered-down overall response. Like other forty-somethings, I enjoy being a consumer, love so much of the popular media culture and vibrancy of our age and consider myself politically astute and 'right-on' on most 'right-on' issues. Yet I find myself strangely caught – too young to become a fully paid-up member of the 'angry brigade', yet when I see an eight-year-old wearing a T-shirt with 'porn star' on it I feel angry and challenged about the issue and in particular the way in which it has become mainstream and so accessible to young people. Surely it is not an inevitable consequence of our de-regulated society? Surely we can stand up against the prevailing anthem of 'it's a free society' and reject the notion that we have all become content and happy in being 'comfortably numb'?[32]

The 3Cs of online danger

Childnet International – the charity I head up – was established in 1995 with the broad mission to *'help make the Internet a great and safe place for children'*. We are fundamentally positive about the opportunities for children using the new generation of communication tools, and believe that it is vital to take a balanced view. We run a range of international programmes which support children and parents to use the Internet for good.[33] However, we are acutely aware of the dangers for children and have broken these down into three main Cs:

CONTENT – *(harmful or illegal or increasingly 'unwanted' content such as SPAM)*

For many parents and carers the initial concern that they have when introducing their children to the Internet is that they will be able to access inappropriate content – pornography in particular. The fact that children are increasingly able to access soft porn in the middle shelves of the newsagent and in most of the 'red-top' newspapers is sadly a part of modern childhood. However, what is challenging about the Internet is that it is more available to young people who otherwise would not have seen it, more extreme and accessible in greater privacy. With the advent of streaming video,[34] and 'cyber-sex' conversation in chat rooms it is more interactive and potentially more addictive.

In the last few years we have seen parental concern move from that of Content to a new anxiety about the potential for harmful

CONTACT – *(meeting up with someone whom you have 'met' online)*

With the continuing number of stories about children being 'groomed' through Internet chat rooms much of the public anxiety has focused on the very real possibility that their children may physically meet up with someone whom they have met through the Internet. Indeed recent research[35] has shown that many children, whilst aware of the dangers, are still wanting to meet up with those whom they have contacted online. Out of all the dangers this is the most serious and I devote a separate section about this danger later.

There is a third C which is also very important to consider when it comes to children and the Internet and it has special relevance to the issue of pornography. It is

COMMERCIALISATION – *(excessive and aggressive commercial marketing)*

Increasingly, there is a blur between content and a lot of advertising. Children's privacy is being invaded by SPAM, scam text messages, viruses and Trojan diallers which divert your dial up access to premium rate services etc. With no 'watershed' or rating service for the Internet, many companies aggressively advertise to younger audiences through pop-ups, SPAM e-mails, and bogus competitions where children are encouraged to supply personal household details.

It is vital to understand that when it comes to pornography online there is an important overlap between these three Cs. Firstly many children and young people can come across pornography by mistake – indeed for those who use an e-mail hotmail account or peer-to-peer file sharing system, it is almost impossible not to be sent pornography attachments, pop-ups or adverts. Recent research co-sponsored by Childnet shows that 57 per cent of young people aged nine to nineteen reported that they had come into contact with pornography online. This contrasts starkly with parent reports where only 16 per cent of believed their children had been exposed to pornography online.[36] (Again an example of this 'digital divide' between generations.)

As other commentators in this book have pointed out, the pornography industry has been the driving force in developing many of the technological advancements on the Internet. This has included video streaming and online payment processes, as well as inventing aggressive marketing pop-ups and banner ads. This 'pushing' of content (as opposed to the customer 'pulling' the content) results in an increasing infringement on our privacy. Sadly children are not immune to this onslaught as they are among the most regular of viewers to the popular commercial sites which these advertisers target.

There is also an overlap between pornography and *Contact* services. Although Internet chat can be used in creative ways to connect children, there are dangers for children using chat unsupervised, especially where adults can use it as a means of establishing inappropriate relationships with young teenagers or children. Sadly paedophiles have recognised the opportunity the Internet affords them to contact children at a safe distance, building up a relationship with them for the sole purpose of persuading them into sexual activity.

The technique which sex offenders use to entice children into sexual activity is known as 'grooming', and this follows a recognised sequence. The adult makes initial contact with the child in a chat room, and once this contact has been established they invite the child into a private area of the chat room to get to know them better.[37] Next in the grooming sequence comes private chat via an instant messaging service, and then e-mail, usually followed up by phone conversations (often on mobile phones) and finally a face-to-face meeting. The grooming process can go on for weeks and months, as it may take this long for the child to feel truly comfortable. The patience of the predator may also be explained partly by the fact that it is not uncommon for them to be grooming several children at the same time. In this way, even if a child begins to feel uncomfortable and breaks off the relationship there are others lined up. One website describes the act of grooming as that of a stranger leaving porn magazines along a path enticing the victim in.[38]

The term 'do you want to Cyber?' is used in some chat rooms to suggest that users move into a private one-on-one chat space so that the users can talk sex for mutual stimulation. It is in this context that the Internet has been called the schoolyard of the twenty-first century. Chat rooms can afford the predator invisible access to children from a safe distance, allowing contact to be made even while the child is using the Internet in the secure surroundings of their own home, even their own bedroom.

Surely something must be done

The challenge of young people coming into contact with a stranger in an unmoderated chat room, and in which pornography was exchanged, came home to Childnet in 2000 when out of the blue we received an e-mail direct to the office from a father who wrote:

> My daughter was contacted starting in February this year by a paedophile whilst using a chat room. He quickly moved to e-mail and shortly afterwards sent her

pornography, purporting to be pictures of himself. My daughter was just 12 at this time. After grooming her for some weeks, he made telephone contact and eventually persuaded her to miss school and meet him. In total, he met her five times and took her back to his flat where she was sexually abused ... I have worked in the computer industry for 18 years, latterly with the Internet, and had no idea what went on in these chat rooms. Surely there is some regulatory body that can make the ISPs monitor at least the teenage chat rooms to make sure kids aren't in danger ... Perhaps you can offer some guidance?

The result of this e-mail and meeting with the parents was that Childnet launched www.chatdanger.com on the steps of the courthouse on the day in which the perpetrator in this case, who was caught by the police, was sentenced. The site generated huge media interest and showcased a way in which the Internet could help educate and inform at a time of public anxiety. However, not everyone agreed with our approach. Someone in America 'webjacked'[39] the site and potential viewers who mistakenly typed www.chat-danger.com were instead sent to a porn site. We also got criticism from some in the industry who felt we were being too negative.

The website was written with the full support of the family and aimed to tell the girl's story in a sensitive, dignified way. Over the last three years we have received over three thousand e-mails through the site's online contact form and have been able to respond personally to hundreds of parents and children who have concerns, giving them advice and reassurance. The website also helped mobilise our challenge to both the government and the industry to review how children were exposed by these new interactive services. In part the campaign helped mobilise the establishment of the Home Office

Task Force on Child Protection on the Internet, of which Childnet is a leading member. This group in turn challenged the government in their review of the Sexual Offences Act to introduce a new criminal offence of online grooming which has now been included. Childnet has also been active in lobbying the chat service providers to take steps to make the chat rooms more child-safe and we welcomed MSN's decision in 2003 to withdraw their chat services.

Mobile porn – a ticking time bomb

A leading research analyst company[40] warned recently that porn on mobile phones was a 'time bomb' and that 'little can be really achieved to control adult content on mobile handsets'. Childnet has challenged the mobile network operators to learn from the lessons of the 'fixed' Internet and ensure that children's rights are respected and parents have greater choice as to what services they can 'opt in' for on their mobile phones.[41] Mobile network operators – many of whom have had to pay excessive sums for the new licences – are desperate to capitalise on new revenue opportunities and exploit adult services on mobile phones. In the UK the mobile operators should be congratulated for establishing a code of conduct for the way in which they will self-regulate themselves and support children.[42] However, companies in other countries are rapidly seeking to roll out adult content services to drive up data revenues including sex channels, dating and flirt SMS services and access to adult dating sites.[43]

We need to be on our guard. In the same way that the porn industry rapidly exploited sophisticated technical and marketing services on the fixed Internet, they are already quick off the mark in developing a whole range of adult services – some of which are called 'Eye Candy'[44] – for consumers willing to pay.

Children and young people are potentially far more vulnerable to mobile porn given that in the UK alone almost 60 per cent of secondary age young people own a mobile phone. Why? Well, in returning to the three Cs of the fixed Internet we can add a further three dangers for children with the net going mobile. (This time three As.)

Away from supervision – Children and young people are extremely private about their mobile. As soon as the third generation phones provide high speed and high quality Internet access, video and interactive services, children will be accessing the world at the bus stop, on the train, in the playground, anywhere that is away from their parents' gaze.

Always on – 'What's the point of having a mobile phone if you keep turning it off?', many children say to their parents who aren't confident in finding the silent ring tone mode! As such, children are vulnerable to responding to messages and content any time of the day and may respond spontaneously without thought or care whilst on the move or showing off with their peers. Children are already receiving abusive and threatening text messages and a recent poll in the UK showed that one in four children report receiving a bullying text message.[45]

Access to Location Based services – Whilst Global Positioning Services (GPS), which help parents track or locate a child, would bring reassurance of safety to parents, there are dangers that tracking services on mobile phones could put children at risk from those who may seek to exploit them or target them. It will shortly be possible to use this technology with multi-user games on mobile handsets with the option of knowing where the person you are playing with is located.

Tenderness in the territory of shame

Whilst software companies are quick to promote their products as tools which can help build community and engender a culture of participation, the Internet has also helped breed isolation and loneliness. I have spoken to many a hassled worker who, having had to respond to countless e-mails during the day, returns home only to spend another four hours online catching up with work, personal e-mails or playing computer games. It's as if they find it hard to cut their umbilical cord to the computer and engage in an offline world. With such addiction to the technology and fractured isolation from the human community how tempting then to find superficial comfort in a world of cyber pornography, with all its choices and levels of erotic attraction. Yet as Martin Amis wrote in *Pornoland*: 'Porn is littered with the deaths of feelings'. Other authors in this book have highlighted that pornography online can lead viewers down a spiral of 'needing' harder and harder pornography to satisfy and stimulate their numbed feelings.

But my children know more about this than I want to!

Helping children understand the nature of pornography online

I want to turn our attention now to what we as parents can do to help support our children on this virtual neon high street – the positive way in which we can engage with children and in doing so challenge ourselves and our society. No simple magic steps here, no crash course in fully protecting your children online, just five short reflections which may help you discuss the issues with your child and help keep them aware of the risks.

1. Try to remember what it was like to be a child

Immersed in such a technological-rich world, it is sometimes so hard to see again the natural world through the eyes of a child – to ask the simple questions again and to try to stand in awe and amazement. But if we stop to do this it can give us hope and a renewed desire not only to cherish children's purity and innocence, but also to recognise again these child-like values in us all, regardless of our age. We are reminded in Matthew 18:3 that 'unless you … become like little children, you will never enter the kingdom of heaven'. It can be a challenge knowing how to talk to children about this issue but it is important not to procrastinate or put it off. Start by trying to view the world from their perspective, think again about the peer pressure they may be under, what exposure to pornography they may have had in different types of media, their level of maturity. Make sure that you let them ask the questions and allow them time to think about their responses and their responsibility without judging.

As I mentioned earlier, children can challenge you about your own honesty and openness. It can be helpful to remember what I call a 'child-interruption test', in which you imagine your child surprising you with the question 'what are you doing, Dad/Mum?' This can be a check for our own eyes and be a powerful motivator to modify our behaviour as well as save possible embarrassment and shame!

2. Treasure and re-visit 'teachable moments'

Following the work we did on chatdanger.com, Childnet staff are often asked by the media to make a comment or be interviewed on a story – often when a child has gone missing or a new piece of research suggests children are in greater danger. I try to be positive, remembering the media's agenda, and will accept the invitation if we can find a 'teachable moment' – that time when you can draw on the story or news article to challenge parents to take more responsibility for their children's well-being. Children are very interested in the lives of other children and can be sensitive and motivated to want to do something about it. Try to seize these moments when children are concerned. It may be to remind them not to give out their personal details online and never to meet up with someone they have been chatting to online. Do not shy away from discussing pornography and Internet danger with your children when it comes up on the *News*, ask them how they feel, whether they feel under pressure from their peers. Use teachable moments to share how you feel too. It is not easy being vulnerable with your children. Clearly you will know your child better than anyone else. Aim the discussion at their level, let them lead. In adolescence it can be harder with teenagers needing more privacy and many finding it harder to articulate their feelings. Parents need to accept these reactions and not judge. If the conversation does not come naturally, try to find other ways to reach out and show your children that you are there to support them.

3. Be careful not to judge

As we discussed in early chapters, children are bombarded by images of soft porn every day. At the bus shelter, while surfing on the net, in the newsagent. Whilst

there are some tell-tale signs that a child may be viewing
unhelpful content (such as the screen is minimised every
time you enter the room!) you need to remember that a
great deal of pornography is 'pushed' to computers
through pop-ups, banner ads and cookies which are
implanted on your machine.[46] Tell your children in
advance that you are able to look at the History folder on
your computer (click on 'History' folder icon) to see what
your children have been looking at. This in itself can help
prevent misuse. If the History folder is repeatedly wiped
this will give you a good opening to ask 'are there
websites which you don't want me to know you've been
looking at?'

If you do find pornography on your computer make
sure you talk about it straight away in a non-threatening,
supportive manner. Remember that for many teenagers
pornography is part of growing up and you will have to
deal with it sometime.

4. Be consistent both offline and online

The FCUK marketing phenomena in which the French
Connection UK company brilliantly and provocatively
used the FCUK misspelling to re-launch its brand, and in
doing so made their T-shirts the pinnacle of 'cool',
typifies the rampant way in which companies are using
sex to sell. It may be more private on the Internet but it is
shouting out on the high street. In talking with your
children about pornography make sure you are
consistent with the online and offline issues. This issue is
not black and white, i.e., what one person finds innocent
or harmless, another finds pornographic. What one
person finds trendy and cool, another may find
provocative and unhelpful. We are sexual beings,
surrounded by images of sex and eroticism, it is part of
being human. However, just because the issues aren't

black and white, let us not make the 'greyness' an excuse for not thinking. Talk to friends about their response and try to find support from other parents who feel like you. (You might be surprised at how many people outside of the church will share your feelings!) Talk as a family about what you will all tolerate, what life-style magazines you will accept, what TV channels you will subscribe to. Zero tolerance can be cool again! Let the words of Philippians 4:8, 'whatever is pure, whatever is lovely, whatever is admirable – if anything is excellent or praiseworthy – think about such things', become a 'screen saver' for every media outlet in your home.

5. *Consider some technical safeguards (dependent on the skills of your child)*

Whenever we at Childnet undertake a parents' seminar,[47] we are always asked by parents what filtering software we recommend. I find this frustrating. As a parent myself I know that I too want a simple answer, a secure baby-sitter tool to keep them safe and occupied. Filtering technology is improving all the time and there are some good products on the market which can help block a lot of pornography as well as help you monitor your children's use and limit the time and services online.[48] But the tough news is that there is no 100 per cent silver-bullet solution to keeping children safe. However hard parents try to 'lock down' their computer with the latest anti-virus and filtering tools, children will come across pornography online, partly because filtering is not 100 per cent guaranteed and the smart kid can often circumvent the filter or switch it off! Children are also accessing the net in a variety of locations from schools, to cyber clubs, libraries, friends' homes and shortly through their mobile phones. Being a good parent – or 'good-enough' parent – is what is more important. No filtering tool will help children distinguish for themselves what is helpful, reliable, fun or useful information. No filter will help them to make good choices themselves as to what media they will access and (importantly) what they will do with the content. There is increasingly a vital role for schools here who need to expand the notion of media literacy to include helping children review the content and services largely accessed out of school.[49] As one commentator puts it 'we need to really be helping our children switch on the filter between their own ears!'[50]

I appreciate that so many parents are time-poor and do not have what they could call the 'luxury' of spending quality time with their children on this issue. Having been part of an inner-city church for the last 20 years I know too that many parents face real economic hardships and a lack of access to the Internet at home means that their children's access is often outside of the home. However, because of the way that children are interacting with the outside world through the Internet, it means that all of us as parents need try to find ways to engage with our children and make time. Any parent who has watched *Finding Nemo* will empathise with Marlon who seeks to protect Nemo from the horrors of the ocean. As Marlon found out, parents *can* help their children, and in doing so learn from children and be challenged afresh about their own views and actions.

A response which won't make us feel bad about doing good![51]

What the church can do?

Whilst practical 'steps' and tips are helpful for individuals and families it is vital that the church makes a strategic response to challenging the powers of pornland. This is uncomfortable for the church which is so often more at home talking about personal individual morality than engaging in the messy world of politics and forming alliances with strange bedfellows. However, helping people think about pornography can be a 'trigger' to engaging in wider issues. At a time when global para- digms are colliding, and when the west is increasingly being seen by the rest of the world as having lost its moral authority, our world is waiting for the church to find its prophetic voice again. Yes the church has been ham- mered and challenged by post-modernist exponents, it has been guilty of double standards and wallowing in the 'grey', but does it not have more to say about such a crucial issue? An issue which impacts so much on the essence of what it means to be a human being? Whilst rampant commercial forces have been free to make wo/ man in their own image, we are in danger of forgetting our life-source and the heart of what it means to be made in the image of God.

Make no mistake, pornography is a sophisticated growing business.[52] Whilst the glamorous air-brushed, perfect body images promise so much, they can reduce the magic of sex to the mechanical and rob us of our humanity. Washed up, hurt and castrated from the love of human tenderness and beauty, pornography destroys. It may be sold and promoted as acceptable and as a sign of a tolerant society, but the legacy of pain, broken relationships, anger and addiction is something which church and social workers are mopping up on a weekly basis.

Getting involved in this issue will challenge the church to have a co-ordinated approach to think outside of the 'box' (or should that be the 'sanctuary'?) and work with other sectors. It will involve re-discovering our prophetic voice again, working with secular partners, as well as learning from and supporting others who share some of our views.

For example

1. Learning from the women's movement, which whilst winning the battle for equality in the sixties and seventies doesn't seem to have had much of an impact on the way big business has, and continues to misrepresent women in advertising today.

2. We need to learn from other faiths about how they have maintained a zero-tolerance view of pornography – whilst rejecting their overall view of the place of women.

3. Like secular commentators such as John Humphrys,[53] we need to re-assess the work of the National Viewers and Listeners Association,[54] who in the seventies sought to stem the tide and exposure of sex on TV yet were mocked as do-gooders and prudes. Who today is taking up the challenge to ensure that the diet of crudity, dumb and vulgar television, served up in the name of high quality 'reality' entertainment, is stemmed?

4. How can we find the strength to pour salt on the open wound of press hypocrisy which on one hand sensationalises and publicises the misery of an individual family whose child has been abused by an online paedophile, but yet appears to take delight in exploiting women and sexualising young people through the publishing of pornography every day?

I am not qualified to speak about how individual church leaders should help members of their churches and wider communities who are struggling with pornography. However, from being a member of a small faith community for the last 20 years I know that I have never heard the word 'masturbation' mentioned in church, never been challenged to boycott a newspaper or brand on the grounds of its dubious marketing strategy, never been encouraged to complain to a TV channel. (In part I must take some responsibility for this having myself been a church leader for four of these years!) However, we must find ways to validate people's experience and hurt and ensure that people can talk about an issue which fundamentally affects our lives and view of each other. There are tremendous opportunities for small group work or finding a 'hook' to work through some of these issues through a survey, questionnaire, mounting a campaign, praying for victims etc.

What I do know is that pastors need support themselves. They need encouragement and practical resources so they can respond to the issues in their own lives and those of their church members, as well as reaching out to others in their wider communities who are damaged from the consequences of pornography. We need space to be able to reflect on the love and compassion of Jesus, who whilst saying little about erotic love (or nudity for that matter) spoke volumes by his words and actions and reminded us on how we should take care of our thoughts and passions, on the way we should love the outcast, how we should be pure in heart and honour our bodies as living sacrifices. What an opportunity to contrast the messy stuff of modernity with the witness of God in human form!

The church has so much to say about the creative mystery of our beings, so much to love about sex. We of all peoples should celebrate what it means to be human because we follow a God who chose to be one! We must not be seen to be merely reactionary, making ripples by throwing proverbial stones into the cesspool from the shore, critical and resentful that we no longer have the voice in society we once did. Rather we should re-double our efforts to get involved in this issue, to act more holistically, to celebrate every representation of our sexuality which is good and wonderful. To find ways to help people of faith – and none – in their search for human and spiritual intimacy.

Returning to Tomi

In conclusion, let us return to our image of the world in children's hands to Tomi who uses the Internet for good. Let us keep this debate in balance, to remember the fantastic, life-changing ways in which the technology can revolutionise children's experiences and knowledge for good. The way in which we can use it to break down barriers and share information. The way in which children can counter the 'dark-side' by producing their own remarkable, imaginative and inspirational work.

Pornography is all around us in our society and a very real danger for children online.

Like the rest of life, there are risks and dangers and as I have noted in this chapter, pornography exists offline too. It's all-pervasive and part of our modern culture. On the Internet it is more private, more anonymous, potentially more addictive, and sadly more dangerous because it can lead to offline harm. Is it an acceptable risk, the inevitable consequence of such a free, creative, global resource? Probably – and I say cautiously – 'yes'. However, the jury is beginning to get restless and we all need to work hard to ensure that the benefits really do outweigh the dangers.

The church *is* responding every day in its work of reaching people caught up in abuse and shame. Our society *will* value the church, not just as a sanctuary, but as an advocate for children if we find the strength to disagree and puncture the 'greyness'. Let us pray we find the courage to speak out and challenge our sex-driven society for the way in which it is harming children.

References

Amis, Martin, *Pornoland* (Thames and Hudson Ltd., 2004)
Berners-Lee, Tim, *Weaving the Web* (Texere Publishing, 1999)

Willing slave or child of God?

David Partington

Introduction

Helping people with addiction problems for 25 years doesn't make it easy to write to someone who has a problem with pornography. I don't only have my experiences to draw on, with other significant issues I've had to deal with, but knowledge from numerous conversations with hundreds of addicts and those who work with them from all over the world. The problem is how to condense, into one chapter, those things which will help you break free into the glorious inheritance God has called you into as his child. What I do know is that if you do have a problem and you're reading this book you have almost certainly taken the first step in dealing with your problem. I say that because the very first step on the road to real freedom is admitting you have a problem in the first place. That's not easy. It's not easy because it means facing up to the reality of those things you're involved with, what you have become and what you have done to others. But, as we will remember again later, that's the best place to begin with as far as Jesus is concerned – acknowledging our weakness and depending on God's grace.

Willing slave?

What is it that turns a king into a slave? What is it that turns a man of God into someone so consumed by the images in his head that he becomes an adulterer and an accomplice to murder? Obviously the images that led King David into the slavery of lust and desire came from being in the wrong place at the wrong time. Having seen a woman, Bathsheba, bathing on a rooftop he fell head-long into a relationship which destroyed a marriage, resulted in one man, Uriah, dying physically and another, King David, dying spiritually as well as various members of both families suffering. Only those Christians who have struggled themselves with sexual sin will have some understanding of the struggle with desire that King David went through. Only those who themselves try to shut out the insidious, all-pervading images, thoughts and emotions will understand how relatively simple it was for him to lose touch with the life of God which he had previously owned and com-municated so powerfully. The power behind the images to corrupt and compel a Christian man or woman to do things they never thought they could possibly do. The lust and desire that an image can evoke that will take them back, again and again, when they would much rather resist. For them the phrase 'Just say no' has a haunting irrelevancy to it. They have tried saying 'No' 10,000 times and still they reach for the mouse knowing that what they are about to look at will demean and spoil them.

It didn't start that way. For some it began way back in their teens, for others it came later in life. For some it came through looking at pictures in the magazines that others handed around. Some picked up an innocent looking periodical and came across a picture or passage that excited them. More recently others didn't even go looking, porn came looking for them. They received one SPAM message too many and thought they would just have a look at what all the fuss was about. One thing led to another but it was all fairly innocuous and they only 'treated' themselves every few weeks just to get some excitement. Then it became more regular, a specific time in the week when their partner was out at a meeting, and eventually daily. Rationalisation and justification about what they were getting into became less and less of an issue as they blocked out the one clear voice that told them they were on a slide and were losing control of the momentum. Then, one day or one dark night, they suddenly woke up to the reality that they were willing slaves.

Slavery for others is something imposed, from outside, by people or circumstances. For them there is the awful truth that they voluntarily surrendered to slavery. They know that the patterns they are involved in are wrong but they don't want to break away. For them the feelings, the emotions, the sexual pleasure is more immediate, more achievable than the peace and the joy that God promises in other ways. They know that the pornography never fully delivers but it's better than going without and facing the emptiness at the core of their being.

Yet they are at war within themselves. They truly want a way out. They long for freedom from the tarnished, sordid existence they continually surrender to. They look every which way for the strength, the conviction, the revelation that will bring the liberty and purity that they know is out there. Eventually they hear God's still small voice and find the will to find the release they have been looking for. They get right with him and enjoy a time of real wholeness and peace. Church is good again, reading the Bible makes sense again, prayer times are worthwhile and relationships with those closest are free of the guilt and shame that once hung over them like a cloak of despair. Then along comes some period of stress and pressure, something which hits their self-esteem and the thoughts return, the images from the past crowd in again. They tell themselves again and *again* that if they surrender to the desires they will degrade and demean themselves and others. They tell themselves that their wife, their husband, deserves better, that they would cheat them if they went back. But the old tapes begin to play, the justification and the rationalisation begin *again*. They deserve some relief, their partner isn't willing enough in bed, no one had found out yet so why should they find out this time? The discomfort of saying no to themselves becomes bigger than their desire to be clean. Their desire for instant gratification becomes larger than their willingness to rejoice in all that God had done in their life. So they go back, even find a way around the systems they had put in place on their PC to stop them going to places on the Internet which are full of promise and depravity. They choose slavery again, knowing that the next time they wanted to break free it will be even harder but it's now that counts, self which rules and, besides, everyone else has some secret sin.

Pornography is one of the most powerful weapons that Satan has ever used to enslave Christians, to neutralise or limit their walk with God. Porn limits and demeans their roles as husbands, wives, fathers and mothers as well as leaders in the church. Involvement in pornography can also lead to an addiction as real and powerful as that experienced by any drug addict or alcoholic. In the same way that addiction came for the drug addict when the drugs controlled them rather than the other way round so there comes a point where the pornography controls the sex addict. If you recoil from thinking that pornography is addictive then I'm sorry but nearly twenty-five years' experience of working with people with life-controlling problems tells me it's true. Pornography can affect every aspect of a person's life and the compulsion to use it can be as addictive as any drug. That's not to demean you or the hundreds of addicts that I have lived and worked with. Every one of them is, just like you, a unique and special person, made in the image of God. That image showed through in the lives of the addicts who became my friends. It showed more times than you would realise. But they were just as caught up in the vicious cycle of surrender to their addiction, breaking free, relapsing, then wanting to be as free again as you. Every one of them wanted *real* freedom, something that would enable them to be free of the slavery to their own compelling lust and desire and that which fed their corrupted and spoiled needs. I have seen, again and again, God transform broken-hearted, broken-spirited, despairing people into those who radiate his love, righteousness and power. I've seen God bring that freedom into being. I've seen him take broken lives and create loving husbands, caring fathers, faithful employees and dynamic church leaders.

The beginning of freedom

If I've learned anything about finding real freedom over the years, for myself as well as others, it's about having a healthy sense of realism about what is really involved. To even begin to suggest that it's easy is so laughable as to be tragic. Most Christians are, regrettably, incredibly naïve about what is involved, probably because they have never been taught the truth about sin. I don't say this in any way to be condemnatory but if you really are going to find the freedom God has for you then a healthy level of realism about the issues involved is crucial. That's what the addicts who found freedom discovered. They were involved in the same difficult cycle of shame, freedom, relapse and shame, freedom ... that you are involved in. What broke the cycle for many was the truth that despite all of that they, like you, were still men and women of God! One of the essential truths that they learned from God was that however devastating their relapses were, he still carried on loving them and that their relapses were often the springboard into renewed life in Jesus. None of that is to excuse those relapses, as they would be the first to admit. But they realised that God's grace is not conditional upon success but on choosing to make use of it. As they struggled to make sense of the Christian life they began to discern certain principles and practices which made a difference but which they had to learn, sometimes over and over again.

One of the first things anyone has to discover about defeating any life-controlling problem is that it's not about being strong. It is all about acknowledging that we are powerless. Admitting such a thing is not easy, it runs contrary to so much of our upbringing in the age in which we have grown up. We've been taught in the world, and in the church, that weakness is bad news. That it is strength and assurance and conviction that are the way to success. All very strange for us as Christians given that Jesus said that his grace and power is more readily available when we are at our weakest (2 Cor. 12:9,10). As we have already reinforced, pornography demeans, enslaves and corrupts that which God intended for good. It destroys, slowly but surely, those whom God created to become like Jesus and it is broken, more often than not, by admitting that we cannot even begin to defeat it. Powerlessness, weakness and surrender, on God's terms, are the gateway to a life of righteousness, hope and victory over those things we choose to be enslaved by. The only way out of our dependency or addiction to porn is to see the situation for what it really is – an offence not only to our status in Jesus but to the One who created and chose us.

Finding your way out is not about working up enough strength to say no but by asking God to reveal himself to you for *who* he is in his holiness and not for what you want from him. What you need is not your own enthusiasm, determination and energy but something in your life which is bigger than the pornography which has enslaved you. That something bigger is God – God the Creator of the universe, the one who holds all things in his hand. God the Father, Son and Holy Spirit. If you're anywhere near acknowledging your own powerlessness before such a God then let me suggest you pray the following words.

> Father, I can't let go of pornography on my own and I need you to come in and be bigger than my desires and lust. You're the biggest, purest, most beautiful person I know. I acknowledge my powerlessness over pornography and I ask you to reveal yourself to me so I can see the evil for what it really is in the light of your holiness and love. I long for something deeper to be right at the centre of all my desires and longings. I ask that you would indwell me like never before with your holiness and as you do so, I want to begin to choose righteousness in all I do. I know this is only the beginning and I truly want to go deeper into you – on your terms and not my own. Amen.

The important truth is that the battle is only just beginning but that battle is about discovering what we are truly created for. You were made to become like Jesus (Rom. 8:29) and what he has planned for your life is really beyond anything you might have imagined. God is far more interested in you knowing him in a deep and intimate relationship than in you having to do anything or achieve anything for him. Ask him to reveal his truth to you and start the process of transformation that he, the God of all creation, has purposed for your life. It will mean a life which is infinitely more fulfilling and deep than anything pornography has to offer.

The core of the problem

Hard core (or soft core) problems need hard core answers. That is a fact which will be very clear to anyone who has tried, more than once, to give up something like pornography. As we've already seen it has invariably resulted in a vicious circle of shame, freedom and relapse which is tiring and depressing. Having tried to give up, again and again, we end up even deeper into our life-controlling problem and feel that there is no hope for ourselves. If we really want 'out' then reality demands that we face the truth that being sorry for being up to our necks in garbage is one thing, facing the truth on God's terms is another. God's truth for us is found in his word which takes us beyond being sorry for ourselves and points to the real facts and the solution.

The life of King David, having shown us how easy it is for a man of God to fall from grace, also confirms God's answer for the most desperate user of porn. Having been presented with the reality of his failure to behave in the way God laid down, David freely acknowledged the central problem at the core of his life and being. The words in Psalm 51, which he wrote following Nathan's exposure of his mistakes, graphically describe that he knew exactly what the problem was.

Have mercy on me, O God,
according to your unfailing love;
according to your great compassion
blot out my transgressions.
Wash away all my iniquity
and cleanse me from my sin.
For I know my transgressions,
and my sin is always before me.
Against you, you only, have I sinned
and done what is evil in your sight ...
(Ps. 51:1-4a)

Here is David's acknowledgement not only of sin but of
how his sin was offensive towards a holy God. Not only
how sin pollutes and corrupts but how it spoils David's
relationship with God. Here is the longing cry, from deep
within his being, of a man who wants to be washed
completely clean so he could be in God's presence again.
And the words, 'Have mercy ...' are so clearly echoed in
the words of the other prodigal: 'Father ... I am no longer
worthy to be called your son.' (Lk. 15:18,19)

Sin is not a word we hear much about these days and it
never ceases to challenge me that I personally am willing
to describe sin as anything but sin. Anger becomes
irritability, breaking the speed limit is justified on the
basis of others doing it, gossip becomes sharing etc. I first
woke up to the real truth of sin in a hotel room in
Eastbourne in southern England. I was on a business trip
and I was very frustrated to find myself with nothing to
read. Reluctant though I was, because I had become a
backsliding Christian, I found myself reading the only
thing I could find to read, a Gideon's Bible. Having found
myself reading the index I, even more reluctantly, found
myself turning the pages to find the reading relating to
'Backsliding' in Psalm 51. 'Defining moment' is a well-
used phrase but reading those verses was one of them for

me. From that point on I not only began to see the reality of sin in my life in a fresh light but found myself on a journey of hope and freedom that is still, over twenty-five years later, profoundly exciting and fulfilling.

I began to see more clearly that sin was that nature within me that has one primary aim – meeting my needs at the expense of all else. Gratifying my desires at the expense of other people and even my own well-being. Sin, in me, says that the only thing that matters in life is meeting my needs and that God is secondary in all other respects. Sin says that I am justified in using everything and anything to make my life as comfortable as possible. Sin in me is right at the heart of preventing me experiencing what God has so wonderfully purposed for my life and my impact on others. Thankfully, as I read Psalm 51, I acknowledged that I was in the same position as David about sin, that I had lost sight of the holiness of God and my real position before him. With acceptance of the purity of God came too the realisation, only vaguely but powerfully, that I had sinned against God. This was actually the beginning of victory and entry into the fullness for my life as I had never known before. I sensed in that hotel room that though such a realisation, if lived out, was going to bring about a lot of discomfort, it heralded a new future. That God could and would not only 'blot out … my iniquity' but would 'Create in me a pure heart [and] Restore to me the joy of [his] salvation and grant me a willing spirit to sustain me.' (Ps. 51:10,12)

As I've already said that was the beginning of the transformation in my life. My hope was not in what I had to do to earn forgiveness but in the knowledge of all that God had done to enable me to come back into an intimate relationship with him – *and stay there.* It was a truth that was graphically reinforced, as I was preparing to write this chapter, from the writings of Oswald Chambers.

If Jesus cannot deliver us from sin, if He cannot adjust us perfectly to God as He says He can; if He cannot fill us with the Holy Spirit until there is nothing that can ever appeal again in sin or the world or the flesh, then He has misled us. But blessed be the name of God, He can! He can so purify, so indwell, so merge with Himself, that only the things that appeal to Him appeal to you.[55]

These words reinforce the truth that as you face sin for what it is you can be free, completely free, of the addiction or dependency on pornography. Why? Because of what God has done, in and through the life of Jesus. Dealing with sin in our own lives is not only about living in that truth but also in recognising how sin comes about in our lives and how God says we can practically defeat it.

The process of sin

The process of sin is described very clearly in what, for me at least, has been a little read passage in James 1:13-15: 'When tempted, no-one should say, "God is tempting me." For God cannot be tempted by evil, nor does he tempt anyone; but each one is tempted when, by his own evil desire, he is dragged away and enticed. Then, after desire has conceived, it gives birth to sin; and sin, when it is full-grown, gives birth to death.' In fact the process is so specifically defined that I am amazed that no one (that I remember) ever emphasised these words as the way to recognise how the central problem of sin in my life is actually activated. Firstly these words make it abundantly clear that God never tempts anyone. I needed to be told this truth because I had lived so much of my Christian life being bitter with God about situations from the past and had used them to justify meeting my needs in the wrong way. If God had made my father stay with me … if God had arranged for me to go to the right school … if God etc. Having established that simple but profound truth that God did not tempt me, I also realised that James goes on to confirm that temptation, in itself, is not sin. The problem comes not with a thought – but what we do with the thought. There are in fact three things we can do, for instance, with a thought that comes into our mind about an attractive member of the opposite sex.

1. Try to ignore the thought completely.
2. Remind ourselves what a wonderful creator God is, to make someone so attractive.
3. Allow our evil desire to kick in and begin to think about them in a way which is anything but helpful.

Options 1 and 2 allow us to get on with life without any undue damage. Option 3 results in sin – unless we take some simple steps which God has shown us to deal with evil desire. The steps we can take are the same ones used by Jesus in the wilderness. Three times Jesus was tempted and three times he responded to the devil's lies by quoting Scripture. Using the same method that the Son of God used strikes me as a pretty solid way of dealing with wrong thoughts. When I began to apply the technique, as I battled to get back into God's way of doing things, I found that it really did work. It wasn't always easy but it worked. I didn't always have a verse which was directly applicable to the particular circumstances I was in but I had a standby which was particularly helpful, 'I have been crucified with Christ and I no longer live, but Christ lives in me' (Gal. 2:20a). Why did this verse in particular help? Because it reminded me about two wonderful truths that God has brought about:

1. That my sin nature (including my evil desires) has been crucified with Christ.
2. That I am not on my own in fighting these thoughts because I am personally indwelt by the Spirit of God with the very presence of Jesus.

The central fact for anyone who is caught up in pornography is that their highly refined evil desires can be defeated. The essential truth is that Jesus has risen from the dead and that his blood can cleanse us from *all* unrighteousness.

Principles to use in defeating sin

Just as there is a process that can, if not stopped, lead to sin and death, so there is a process that we can use to go from sin to life. 'You were taught, with regard to your former way of life, to put off your old self, which is being corrupted by its deceitful desires; to be made new in the attitude of your minds; and to put on the new self, created to be like God in true righteousness and holiness' (Eph. 4:22-24). These verses set out the way that anyone can defeat the desire to go back to porn. As ever, with the word of God, it's quite simple in that we can:

• Choose to 'put off' the old behaviour, attitudes or practices
• Choose to have the attitude of our minds renewed
• Put on the new self created to be like God in true righteousness and holiness

I make no apology in unwrapping this process, of defeating sin, by starting at the end rather than at the beginning. It seems to me that the greatest hope of all, when it comes to fighting against the over-inflated thoughts and evil desires that constantly crowd our mind, is to accept the awesome truth that as we deal with sin on God's terms we actually begin to become like him in 'true righteousness and holiness.' Have you truly grasped what these words are saying to *you*? Whatever your situation at the moment, no matter how many times you have tried and failed to be what God wants you to be, his call to *you* is still the same – become like Jesus. Doesn't this help to put the sordid, highly inflated, exploitative world of pornography into perspective? Which will you seek? That world, or do you want to become like Jesus and to enter into the place where you are, like Jesus, totally dependent upon your Father?

Let's go back to the beginning, to choose to actively and deliberately 'put off' the sins associated with pornography. But you say, 'I've tried so often to stop and it still hasn't worked fully.' Like others you have found that simply stopping doing something leaves a vacuum into which a thousand other images can flood in. But the words here from God say that stopping is only part of the process laid down by him. He says don't only 'put off' but go further. Put off *and* have your mind renewed as well. Renewal of our mind can be done in so many different ways. In the midst of trying to deal with evil desires around porn it can be in deliberately choosing to read a Christian book which feeds our minds with the truths of God. It can be in listening to a worship song that speaks to us about the holiness and love of God. Or, as we have already reminded ourselves, we can read, or quote to ourselves, a favourite Scripture which washes our mind and leaves far less room for evil desires. Still these are just the first two steps which are only part of the process of defeating sin effectively. So often we need to follow up the decision to stop and fill our minds with the truth and, finally, to do something, to 'put on'. That chapter in Ephesians has two very clear examples of how a liar or a thief can 'put on' something that will lead them to be like God in true righteousness and holiness. For the liar it was about putting on by deliberately going out of their way (regardless of the consequences!) to speak the truth. The thief on the other hand put on his new identity by working with his hands in order to earn something to share with those in need. For the person who struggles with pornography the act of putting something on in its place can be worked out in different ways. It can be in doing something practical in the house when they would normally go into the place where they look at porn. It can be all about doing DIY for yourself or someone else in need. It can be in reading the Bible or another positive book. The possibilities are endless and when you run out of ideas ask the God who is full of ideas not least because he wants you to become more like him!

In terms of moving freely into what God has purposed for your life there's one more issue that is set out in Psalm 51 that will bring increasing hope and victory in defeating porn. It's a place where you have probably been many times before. It's that condition described as having 'a broken spirit and a contrite heart'. It's an uncomfortable place to be but it's also a condition which is gloriously important to God. The truth is that we can bring nothing more beautiful to God than our broken and contrite heart as a living sacrifice to him. It's a heart broken by the depravity of sin and the damage it has caused those closest to us as well as our own physical and spiritual being. It's a contrite heart that recognises that we have offended God by living a life which is far less than that which he created us for. When we come on these terms we come to him without any conditions, any demands or anything of value in our self. It is a place of utter surrender and it doesn't matter how many times we've done it before. A broken and a contrite heart is *always* acceptable to God. A quote I came across recently, in a newsletter for Christians in the caring professions, sums up what happens when we come to God with this sacrifice.

> Today our world may be infinitely complex and sophistica-ted, but God is still the same and fundamentally men and women have not changed. God still looks for those with a broken spirit and contrite heart. A broken spirit has nothing to do with timidity or fear; rather the reverse. Those who have truly yielded to God do not fear. They are not worried about their reputation or what others may think about them. The most important thing for them has become to know God. They are at peace with God because they have given up struggling. Like (King) David, they have come to see that they are sinners and nothing they do will make it right with God against whom they have sinned. They no longer trust themselves but have put their hope fully in the grace and mercy of God. They have come to understand the magnificent truth that Paul wrote to the Roman Christians, 'If God be for us, who can be against us?' They do not look for material comfort or prosperity as a mark of God's favour, but have come to know God in a way that increasingly means they take little thought for themselves. They understand what the psalmist meant when he said that he would rather be a doorkeeper in the house of the Lord than have the greatest wealth the world could offer but be without Him.[56]

Walking the 'talk'

Seeing the transformation that takes place when people break free from porn is something very special. You can see the reality of that inner breakthrough in their face and their whole demeanour and their words are so full of hope. They all say similar things; about the 'weight' that has dropped off their shoulders, about feeling 'clean' again, of the restored relationships and the sense of hope they enjoy. More than anything they speak about being right with God and knowing that he really is helping them in their day-to-day walk. Little can compare with such times of blessing and they can go on for a long time but only a spiritually naïve person would suggest that those times of living on the mountaintops can last for all time. Temptation does come again, often when we least expect it, and it's almost guaranteed when we have convinced ourselves that the problem is all over. In fact the most disturbing thing I hear from the lips of those who have experienced freedom from life-controlling problems is, 'It's all over now, God has set me completely free.' The implication behind their words being that they will never have a problem with this issue ever again. It's then that I have to find the words that will face them with a sense of reality whilst keeping them rejoicing in the truth that God has set them free and all the resources of heaven are available for them to remain free. So too the words have to be communicated that build into them the sensitivity to the temptations which will edge into their minds, especially in this age of 'full frontal' excess that we live in. The need for them to be aware of the subtle reality of the images, the emotions and the feelings that can creep back in, especially when the first flush of being clean and feeling whole has begun to fade. I say all this not to condemn or to be negative for the sake of it but in the sure and certain confidence that realism about guerrilla attacks from the enemy are best dealt with when we are prepared for them. Yet, all the time, there is the blessing of telling them that God has provided so many spiritual and practical ways to help anyone who wants to walk in his grace, power and freedom – for the rest of their lives. So many ways in fact that there are not enough pages in a thousand books to communicate them. There are some basics however which are well worth while communicating.

Practical spiritual ways of maintaining freedom

Be accountable

One of the most valuable things we can do to stay free of temptation to porn, as well as actually returning to it, is to choose to be accountable to someone else. To go to another person we respect, and acknowledge our problem and ask them if they will help to put in place around us a framework of regular contact during which there will be, on both sides, an environment and relationship of absolute honesty and vulnerability. You are asking them for even more! You are asking for them to be confrontational, hopefully in a gracious and gentle manner, in challenging any sign of spiritual naivety or complacency. They are people who are not only caring, gracious and understand human weakness better than most but who are willing to ask intrusive, searching and even embarrassing questions. Questions which bring you face-to-face with the truth about where you're really at on the road to real freedom. You are asking them to be open to the Spirit of God, for you, in a way that few people are used to being. Most people who have tried to break free acknowledge that accountability like that is a key factor in staying clean. Just knowing that they had to talk regularly and very openly with someone about their life and progress was vital in preventing them from slipping back into clicking the mouse. However finding someone with the right level of experience is often far from easy. One person I have had the privilege of advising, the leader of a church, wrote, 'General pastoral support has not been good. My experience has been that fellow professionals and the average minister or pastoral supporter do not respond supportively in any way, they do not know what to do and just ignore your vague plea for help.'

I have quoted this leader because it is vitally important, to you, to know it might not be easy to find exactly the right person. What I am sure of is that God is not going to leave you high and dry if this paragon of expertise does not readily appear. Start looking and ask God to show you who you should ask to be accountable to. Start with your minister/pastor because they need to know you have a problem anyway. Show them the criteria/job description of the person you need to meet with and ask if they will do it. If you don't get the answer you need then ask them to reconsider their response. Make it clear that you want to be accountable to someone and, if it can't be them, ask them to work with you at finding the right person. If you still hit a brick wall then ask them to pray and ask God again who can help. If all else fails throw yourself on God's mercy and choose to be accountable to the Holy Spirit of God. What I mean by this is to keep to the basics described in this chapter and enjoy looking to God to show you the way forward.

'How often do you need to see someone you have asked to be accountable to?' is a frequently asked question. My own view is that if you really are serious about staying free it needs to be as often as the person who has agreed to help you can make it. It probably needs to be at least once a week to begin with simply because you need to talk through who you are, how you got involved with pornography and what you are doing to deal with it. The frequency of meetings can then be adjusted to reflect the progress you make. Never be afraid to ask if you can meet more often, if only for a while, if you experience problems you cannot deal with alone. And always remember that someone can only help you as far as you are prepared to go. If you are not prepared to be open and honest about the real situation you are involved in then no one can help you, no matter how experienced, or otherwise, they are.

Openness with our nearest and dearest

Even more scary than telling your minister that you have a problem is telling your wife or husband. Yet the import-ance of this step cannot begin to be over-emphasised. This relationship has to be based on absolute trust and openness and if it is not the enemy will use the situation to spoil and destroy that relationship. If they are not specifically aware of your use of pornography (and often they are but, like you, dare not confront it) then they will know deep down that there is a problem anyway. Those who love us the most are always those who recognise that something is not what it should be in our lives. Will they feel cheated when you tell them? Yes, desperately so! But the alternative is to continue to cheat them anyway by refusing to tell them about something in your life which has come between you and them. Of course their initial reaction will be one of confusion, disgust and even a sense of their own failure and inadequacy. But your own open confession and repentance can be the doorway to a deeper relationship with them than ever before. One person wrote, after telling his wife, 'The more I told her, the closer we got.' Once over their initial shock, few partners will choose not to respond positively to your vulnerability and will very often work with you towards a deeper sense of intimacy than you ever knew before. If it takes time for that to happen, as it will almost certainly do, then surely they deserve the grace, that Jesus always showed, in giving them all the time they need to come to terms with the deep sense of hurt they feel. Responding in the right way to their coldness or rejection of you will be used by God to not only bring them to a place of forgiveness but to help you in the fight against pornography. Treating others in the same servant spirit that Jesus has, even when we are desperate for love and understanding and even sexual tenderness, can be unbelievably liberating and healing for us if we draw our strength and patience from God's grace and love.

Finally, on the subject of accountability, the best people to be accountable to are those who know their own weakness to sin. I write this not only to help you discern the right person to be accountable to but to plant the seed in your mind that one day God may well want to use you and the difficulties you have been through to help others break free.

Maintain a transparent lifestyle

Dealing with temptation to go on the web to find the wrong material can also be dealt with at a very practical level. You can guard against evil, on the web or anywhere else, in some very simple and practical ways.

- Stop using the computer, at least for a time, completely
- Keep the door open when you are using your computer and turn the screen or your desk around so anyone coming in can see what you're looking at
- Don't use any computer when others are not around e.g. late at night

- Put filters or contact barrier software on your computer
- Use systems like Covenant Eyes via care.org.uk/anon and other Christian resources which help you to be accountable to at least one other person about what you watch/access on the Internet
- Be careful what you read and what you watch on the TV. Plan your programming carefully. If you do find you are watching something suggestive then walk away from it
- Clean out all the material on your computer and, if necessary, get a completely new hard drive
- Get rid of any potentially problematic material stashed away in the house, garage, shed, workplace – anywhere
- Change your patterns of behaviour. Work out those times when you are most in danger and devise alternative strategies to fill that time with those things that bless others as well as yourself. Dig the garden, go jogging, decorate the house, etc.
- Get involved in group support programmes like 'Freedom in Christ' or 'Lifeshapers' where you will meet people like yourself who want to deal with their problems
- Ask yourself, if you drink alcohol, if it can make you more vulnerable to pornography. If it does either give it up or be careful when you use it
- Go to church as often as you can. Avoiding church is often a sign that we are slipping into deeper sin. When you are seeking to walk on the well-travelled road of recovery getting all the spiritual input you can is very, very helpful.

Finally, read your Bible and pray morning and night even if it is only for a few minutes. If other Christians can afford the dubious luxury of only doing so when the Spirit leads, then few of those breaking free and staying free can afford to do so. If others can get close to God by praying as and when they 'think about it' in the middle of very busy, pressurised lives, then God bless them. All I know is that I and others, and especially those with life-controlling problems or tendencies, have benefited immeasurably from the daily discipline of spending a 'quiet time' with the one who loves them and wants an intimate relationship with them. Bible 'readings' abound and translations like 'The Message' bring a whole new dynamic to knowing more of God's word to get us through the pressures of daily life. Would we think that we could build a relationship with the most exciting person in our lives any other way than by spending time listening to them and telling them our deepest needs?

All of these guidelines to enjoying a transparent lifestyle are only as helpful as *you* want them to be. You can find ways around systems on your computer which are designed to help you avoid porn, for instance, but the only loser is yourself. You needn't go to church, read the Bible or do any of the other things, but unless you find ways of filling your life with what God holds to be important pretty soon the enemy will fill it with garbage. The decision is yours and the will to know God by what you read and what you *do* is your choice and no one else's.

Always be aware, especially when you are doing well, that relapse can come at any time. Being aware of that is not to deny God's grace, that is what has kept you free. However it is realistic to acknowledge that we have an enemy who wants us to fail, as well as bearing in mind that we have that sin nature, which is very subtle, that can draw us back to the garbage. If the Bible is realistic then we might as well be! 'So, if you think you are

standing firm, be careful that you don't fall! No temptation has seized you except what is common to man. And
God is faithful; he will not let you be tempted beyond
what you can bear. But when you are tempted, he will
also provide a way out so that you can stand up under it.'
(1 Cor. 10:12,13).

Again it's important to acknowledge that doing things
God's way is not easy but it is easier than *not* doing things
God's way. Sometimes it can seem as if we are, at worst,
slipping back and, at best, walking up a very steep hill
with no sign of the top through the mist. I was given the
following words (for which I have no source) when I was
going through some tough issues in life and they
wonderfully describe the way we sometime feel *and* the
glorious hope we have in knowing God best in the hard
times.

> Pressed out of measure and pressed to all length
> Pressed so intensely it seems beyond strength
> Pressed in the body and pressed in the soul
> Pressed in the mind till the dark waters roll
> Pressed by foes and pressure from friends
> Pressure on pressure, till life nearly ends.
> Pressed into knowing no helper but God
> Pressed into loving the staff and the rod
> Pressed into liberty where nothing else clings
> Pressed into faith for impossible things
> Pressed into living a life in the Lord
> Pressed into loving a Christ life outpoured.
> (Anon)

The blessing of spiritual authenticity

One of the most amazing privileges of being set free from
a life-controlling problem is to know one's absolute need

of God. To be so desperate for his touch, to long to know more of him, is an exquisite necessity that few these days seem to want. It never ceases to amaze me that those who experience that need, and the blessing that goes with it, are often those who have either suffered the most (often as the result of circumstances beyond their control) or those who have wandered furthest from God but have found that they need and want him more than anything else in life. Yet why should we be so surprised that God would bless us so? His word to us says seek me and I *will* be found (see 1 Chr. 28:9). He also shouts at us that those who seek him will lack *no good thing* (Ps. 34:10). The list of what God promises those who seek him goes on and on and simply reinforces that anyone, no matter how messed up, can have all of God that he has purposed for them. What an amazing privilege that can only come from a Creator God who takes broken, burnt-out, sinful lives and promises them resurrection newness – full of himself.

I've had the privilege of seeing others, previously living depraved and sinful lives, who, when they realised their need of God, and came to him on his terms, moved into an entirely new and profound sense of his largeness and just how much he wanted them to enjoy him as well as worship him. They found out that choosing to be a disciple of Jesus not only transformed their whole way of thinking about life but carried with it the promise of being Jesus to others. What a turn-around. The call from God is to go from the depths to the heights, not as some plaster saint with a crooked halo, but to attain to the maturity (and humanity) of Jesus. Isn't this what *you* have always been searching for? To be at the very centre of the source of holy love and to be used by that source of love to bless others? Is there a greater privilege? I think not. Is it easy? No way! The reality is that living life on

God's terms is tough. In fact it doesn't get any tougher as the lives and experience of Jesus and other people in the Bible remind us. So when you do tell God that you want *all* that he has for you don't do it without counting the cost. The results are priceless as one of my heroes in faith, Selwyn Hughes, puts it: 'Becoming a disciple means we commit ourselves to long-term obedience, whereupon we find ourselves immersed in the glorious love and life of the Trinity – Father, Son and Holy Spirit. Then we embark on the continued teaching and training that makes us mature.'[57]

The Bible categorically says that God has given *you* all you need 'for life and godliness' (2 Pet. 1:3). How has he done it? Through his divine power and through your knowledge of him who called you through his own glory and goodness! So the question when you're tempted to go back to the pigsty is what do *you* want? The old sordid existence or the new divine life? You have to ask the question because going back will always be an option until you enter fully into the new life with God in heaven. That's how much he loves you – enough to respect your choice to choose or deny him. Living in the truth and reality of the new life is about reinforcing and living out that which he has purposed rather than what our sinful nature desires. When a group of us were talking about writing this book, Lyndon Bowring shared with me a vital verse about choosing the right things, 'Teach me your ways, O Lord, that I may live according to your truth! Grant me purity of heart, that I may honor you. With all my heart I will praise you, O Lord, my God. I will give glory to your name forever' (Ps 86:11,12, New Living Translation). It's a verse that we would all do well to ask God to write as a prayer deep in our hearts. That we will go on seeking to walk with him in his truth with a deep passion which dismisses and rejects anything which is not of him. And, as we choose to be holy, that our lives will increasingly bring glory to his name as we know more of Jesus.

> Jesus, my all in all Thou art,
> My rest in toil, my ease in pain,
> The medicine of my broken heart
> In war my peace, in loss my gain,
> My smile beneath the tyrant's frown
> In shame my glory and my crown.
>
> In want my plentiful supply,
> In weakness my almighty power,
> In bonds my perfect liberty,
> My light in Satan's darkest hour,
> My help and stay whene'er I call,
> My life in death, my heaven, my all.

(Charles Wesley, 1707–1788)

Reference

Chambers, Oswald, *Here is God's Plenty* (Nova Publishing, 1990)

Notes

1 John Donne, *Poems and Prose.*
2 D.H. Lawrence, 'Pornography and Obscenity'.
3 Michael D. Mehta and D.E. Plaza, 'Content analysis of pornographic images available on the Internet'.
4 J.M. Boice, *Foundations of Faith.*
5 Lord Longford, *Pornography: The Longford Report.*
6 Paraphrased from Nigel Williams' *False Images.*
7 See References for this chapter.
8 *Third Way,* March 2004, p. 18. Used by permission.
9 Names and some details have been changed in this chapter to preserve anonymity.
10 In comparison to figures for e.g. Chlamydia or genital warts, HIV incidence in these countries is minuscule. It is Africa, Asia and now Russia that is ravaged by HIV.
11 Richard Griffiths, *Art, Pornography and Human Value.*
12 Final Report of the Attorney General's Commission on Pornography (Rutledge Hill Press, 1986).
13 Quote from Earl Wilson from *Sexual Sanity* (IVP, 1984), p. 78.
14 Susan Griffin, *Pornography and Silence.*
15 Rollo May, *Love and Will.*
16 See Catherine Itzen and Corinne Sweet, 'What should we do about pornography?', *Cosmopolitan,* November (1989), p. 8.
17 Dolf Zillman and Jennings Bryant, 'Pornography, sexual callousness and the trivialisation of rape', *Journal of Communication* 32 (1985), pp. 10–21.

[18] John Court, 'Pornography and Rape: Promise and Fulfillment', Research report to the Criminology Research Council, Canberra, 1977.

[19] Quoted by Michael Laslett in 'Men's fantasies and actions controlled by pornography' from the Minneapolis Hearings, Everywoman, 1988, p. 127.

[20] Catherine Itzen (ed.), *Pornography and Sexual Violence in Pornography,* (OUP, 1993).

[21] Interview with Ted Bundy by Dr James Dobson, 25 January 1989.

[22] See Heritage Foundation site at: http://www.heritage.org/Research/Welfare/abstinencereport.cfm.

[23] A. Cooper, D.E. Putnam, L.A. Planchon and S.C. Boies, 'Online sexual compulsivity: getting tangled in the net', *Sexual Compulsivity and Addiction; the journal of treatment and prevention*, 6 (1999), pp. 79–104.

[24] Adapted and used with the permission of Prodigals International.

[25] John Court, *Pornography – A Christian Critique.*

[26] Tomi and his parents have given permission for me to use this story and photo (which I took).

[27] Increasingly government departments are using the phrase 'digital opportunities' which is seen as more positive than 'digital divide'.

[28] 'The other digital divide' and 'life-literate' are phrases I believe were coined by Anne Collier, editor/president of NetFamilyNews.org, a US-based newsletter and nonprofit organisation that helps parents understand and be engaged in their children's use of technology.

[29] Tim Berners-Lee, *Weaving the Web.*

[30] A young woman at my church recently wore such a T-shirt during a Sunday morning service, but to my knowledge no one complained. My partner and I were at a loss as to what to do.

[31] *Sunday Times* newspaper magazine, August 2004.

[32] Pink Floyd brilliantly used this phrase as a title for a song on the 1979 'The Wall' album which eloquently espouses a theme for a generation.

[33] See www.childnet-int.org for full details including our award winning education and awareness resources such as www.kidsmart.org.uk and www.net-detectives.org and global academy programme www.childnetacademy.org

[34] Video played over the Internet.

[35] Recent research by the London School of Economics shows that many children whilst being aware of the dangers are still wanting to meet up with those whom they have met online. See www.children-go-online.org

[36] The survey 'UK Children Go Online' presents findings from a national, in-home, face-to-face survey of 1,511 young people aged nine to nineteen and a written questionnaire to 906 of their parents. Funded by an Economic and Social Research Council grant under the e-Society Programme.

[37] Although there is no blueprint for the language of grooming, there are some characteristics of the communication which may give a clue to the true nature of a new online 'friendship'. Such warning signals could be indicated from the 'friend' constantly asking the child for information before telling anything about themselves, by their sending a lot of messages, asking for personal contact details, asking private questions and asking for photographs. These more obvious characteristics of grooming would be accompanied by less obvious traits, such as showing an excessive interest in the child or the giving of a lot of flattery. Given that all this could be contained in communications stretching over a period of months, and that the initiator is conscious of the need for subtlety in this delicate intricate manipulation, these warning signals would not necessarily be obvious.

[38] See www.websafecrackerz.com and click on 'blah, blah, blah' section. This website was produced by MSN with support from Childnet and other charities.

[39] This is the business of hackers hijacking legitimate web pages or setting up similar sounding names for legitimate websites and redirecting users to pornography sites or sites set up for fraudulent business schemes.

[40] Current Analysis report, June 2004 (source: http://www. theregister. co.uk/2004/06/10/mobile_adult_content/).

[41] See Childnet's paper 'Children and Mobile Phones: An Agenda for Action' at www.childnet-int.org/publications and the GSMA conference speech that I gave in Cannes in February 2004 at http://www.childnet-int.org/publications/presentations.aspx

[42] See www.o2.co.uk/abouto2/ukcodeofpractice.html

[43] In Japan young people are already using 3G phones to access dating sites leading to many cases of children then getting into child prostitution and being sexually abused. See Childnet's report on its ground-breaking conference in Japan in March 2003 at www.childnet-int.org/mobiles

[44] As if you take your phone out of your pocket and consume pornography in much the same way as you would quickly enjoy a sweet!

[45] Source www.nch.org.uk/itok

[46] Cookies are pieces of information generated by a web server and stored in the user's computer, ready for future access. They are implemented to allow user-side customisation of web information. For example, cookies are used to personalise web search engines, to allow users to participate in contests (but only once!), and to store shopping lists of items a user has selected while browsing through a virtual shopping mall.

[47] See www.kidsmart.org.uk/parents. There are a number of interactive parents' resources here including a module on helping your children with pornography.

[48] For a good review see www.kidsmart.org.uk/parents or www.getnetwise.org which lists hundreds of products.

[49] Most schools don't allow children to access interactive services such as chat rooms. Furthermore most schools have filtered and protected environments. It's understandable and good that schools have this so called 'air-bag' environment but do encourage your school to help children understand the wider issues of unreliable content, harmful and indeed illegal content, online stranger-danger issues and how to behave online when their parent or teacher isn't looking.

[50] Parry Aftab, security, privacy and cyberspace lawyer, as well as an author and Internet child safety expert.

[51] In our post-modern age it's so unfashionable to talk about morals and indeed can be an affront to others to tell them what is good for them! This is a play on words on the famous advertising line which accompanied the first Emmanuelle porn films of the 1970s which used the catch-line, 'At last – a film that won't make you feel bad about feeling good'. How can the church reclaim authority to tell others what is bad for them?

[52] John Walsh's article on 'Porn in the UK' published in the *Independent* Newspaper in August 2004 reviews the way in which pornography has become mainstream and the forthcoming expansion of sex shops coming to a high street near you.

[53] John Humphrys, speaking at the Edinburgh International Television Festival in August 2004, said that the sixties campaigner Mary Whitehouse had been right when she said television was on a downward moral spiral and that today channel bosses had allowed the genre of television reality shows to turn 'human beings into freaks' and erode the distinction between public and the private in British life with their 'mind-numbing witless vulgarity'.

[54] Now called Media Watch.

[55] Oswald Chambers, *Here is God's Plenty*.

[56] Derek Munday, 'Christians in Caring Professions' Newsletter, March 2004.

[57] Selwyn Hughes, *Every Day with Jesus*, July–August 2004.

Main Websites and contacts

CARE, 53 Romney Street
London SW1 3RF
020 7227 4710

www.care.org.uk/anon
www.carelinkuk.org
www.Childnet-int-org
www.kidsmart.org.uk

www.getnetwise.org
www.covenanteyes.com
(and via the CARE
website)

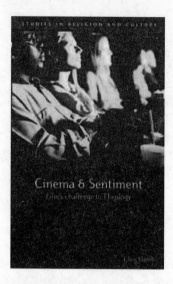

Cinema and Sentiment: Film's Challenge to Theology

Clive Marsh

What do films do to people? What do people do with films?

All film-watching happens within a cultural context. Exploring cinema-going as leisure activity and by comparing film-watching with worship, Clive Marsh demonstrates aspects of the religious function of film-watching in Western culture. Through a variety of case-studies, including a look at the films of Robin Williams and the Coen brothers, Marsh's study shows how film-watching as a regular practice contributes to the shaping of human living.

Engaging with rapidly changing social and religious behaviour patterns in Western culture, *Cinema and Sentiment* suggests a need to recover a positive sense of 'sentiment', both in theology and film. In his final chapter he offers to church leaders, students of theology and film studies, and all those with an interest in contemporary culture some very practical suggestions

'Marsh is right! Popular movies do more than mindlessly entertain or illustrate truth already known … By considering the affective nature of the reader/viewer, *Cinema and Sentiment* explores the central point of connection between theology and film.'
Professor Robert K. Johnston, Author of *Reel Spirituality*

ISBN: 1-84227-274-8

Available from your local Christian bookshop or
www.WesleyOwen.com

Mission Implausible: Restoring Credibility to the Church

Duncan MacLaren

It is commonly agreed that the churches of Europe are in crisis – but why? How can we explain their dramatic decline over the past four decades? In particular, why do contemporary people struggle to believe? And how might the churches address this crisis of credibility? Are there already signs of hope? What can tenacious forms of religion teach the churches as they go about their task of mission?

Mission Implausible tackles these questions using the tools of sociological analysis. It argues that much of the blame for church decline is misplaced and that a broader explanation is required which sets the current crisis within a historical and sociological perspective. Written for church leaders, theologians, students of theology and sociology and all those concerned with Christian mission, *Mission Implausible* explores a range of strategies aimed at rebuilding a social climate favourable to Christian belief.

'MacLaren forces us to re-examine the rhetoric of much of the contemporary discussion on mission and emerging Church in Britain … This is quite simply a crucial and timely book.'
Pete Ward, Lecturer, King's College, London

'A wide-ranging and balanced guide for all who are perplexed by the decline of Christendom and the paradoxes of secularization.'
David Martin, Emeritus Professor of Sociology, London School of Economics

'Mandatory reading for serious practioners of mission. Nothing less.'
Andrew Walker, Canon Professor of Theology, Culture and Education, King's College, London

ISBN: 1-84227-295-0

Available from your local Christian bookshop or www.WesleyOwen.com

Mysticisms East and West: Studies in Mystical Experience

Theodore Gabriel and Chris Partridge (eds)

Mysticism is proving to be the chosen type of religion for future generations of believers in the West. As traditional institutional religion continues to decline, mystical thought is celebrated as a vital, subversive alternative. Whilst this shift is not new, an increasing number of westerners are turning East because they find the fundamentally mystical thought of Asian religious traditions appealing.

Mysticisms East and West examines the worldwide phenomenon of mystical experience across the world religions. In examining both Christian and non-Christian expressions of mysticism, this unique volume brings together a number of prominent evangelical scholars to analyse the central historical, cultural and theological issues. Beginning in the East, these studies in mystical experience gradually move to the West and to both Christian and postmodern philosophical mysticism before concluding with a number of philosophically reflective essays examining the implications and nature of mysticism.

ISBN: 1-84227-092-3

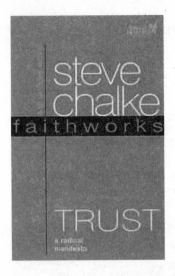

Trust:
A Radical
Manifesto

Steve Chalke and
Anthony Watkis

There are countless commentaries on the reasons for the erosion of trust in society today. The government, the media, the royal family, the church, the police, the law lords, and many more have tumbled from their pedestals. But rather than a catalogue of reasons for failure this is a manual for reconstruction. Steve Chalke examines practical ways through which trust can be built in 21st century society and asks hard questions of government and church as they both strive to become more trusted by the public and each other.

'Timely, thought provoking and debate-inducing. I commend it to you as a tool for change.'
Joel Edwards, Evangelical Alliance

'This book shows how we need to work together to repair the damage caused in the last few decades by the loss of trust.'
Andy Reed MP, Labour

'Steve's book will inspire us all.'
Caroline Spelman MP, Conservative

'Steve Chalke provides a refreshing alternative to the lazy cynicism which says that engaging with the political world is a waste of time … It is time to take on the cynics, and this book provides us with a road map.'
Steve Webb MP, Liberal Democrat

Steve Chalke MBE is the founder of Oasis Global and the Faithworks Movement as well as an author, broadcaster, speaker and the senior minister of the church.co.uk centre, Waterloo.

Anthony Watkis is a graduate of The London School of Theology. He is a professional writer and works with Oasis UK.

ISBN: 1-85078-586-4

Available from your local Christian bookshop or www.WesleyOwen.com